Gendered Citizenship

Oxford Studies in Gender and International Relations

Series editors: J. Ann Tickner, University of Southern California, and Laura Sjoberg, University of Florida

Gendered Citizenship

*Understanding Gendered Violence
in Democratic India*

NATASHA BEHL

OXFORD
UNIVERSITY PRESS

Oxford University Press is a department of the University of Oxford. It furthers
the University's objective of excellence in research, scholarship, and education
by publishing worldwide. Oxford is a registered trade mark of Oxford University
Press in the UK and certain other countries.

Published in the United States of America by Oxford University Press
198 Madison Avenue, New York, NY 10016, United States of America.

Library of Congress Cataloging-in-Publication Data
Names: Behl, Natasha, author.
Title: Gendered citizenship : understanding gendered violence
in democratic India / Natasha Behl.
Description: New York : Oxford University Press, 2019. |
Series: Oxford studies in gender and international relations |
Includes bibliographical references and index.
Identifiers: LCCN 2018057796 (print) | LCCN 2019004996 (ebook) |
ISBN 9780190949433 (Updf) | ISBN 9780190949440 (Epub) |
ISBN 9780190949426 (hardcover) | ISBN 9780197576908 (paperback)
Subjects: LCSH: Women—Violence against—India. | Sikh women—Violence
against—India. | Women—Social conditions—India. | Sikh women—Social
conditions—India. | Women—Legal status, laws, etc.—India. |
Citizenship—Social aspects—India. | Democracy—Social aspects—India.
Classification: LCC HV6250.4.W65 (ebook) | LCC HV6250.4.W65 B438 2019 (print) |
DDC 362.88082/0954—dc23
LC record available at https://lccn.loc.gov/2018057796

Dedicated to my parents, Ashok and Jass Behl;
without you I am nothing, I do nothing.

CONTENTS

ACKNOWLEDGMENTS

I have a debt that I can never repay to the research participants in Punjab, India, for their generosity and insights. Without their stories, this project would be impossible. I have done my best to keep faith with their stories. I have also done my best to keep faith with Jyoti Singh's story and the stories of the countless unnamed victims of gendered violence who inspired this research.

I am extremely grateful to my mentors, who taught me what it means to stick with a problem, to dwell on its complexities, and to push even further. Foremost among these are Raymond Rocco, Caroline Heldman, Rita Dhamoon, and Anna Sampaio, who through their exemplary scholarship and patient guidance have made the undertaking of this project both a challenge and a pleasure. I am especially grateful for their help in navigating life inside and outside of academia. I should also note that the concept of exclusionary inclusion that I advance in the book is also used by Raymond Rocco (2014). The initial formulation of this concept emerged from collaborative discussion, teaching, and writing.

To my mentors and teachers at Smith College, who inspired me to start this academic journey, I would like to say thank you. Thank you to Ambreen Hai and Tandeka Nkiwane for being my role models. Your strength inspired me to start my journey on this path. I would also like to thank Andy Rotman for encouraging me to conduct research on Sikhs in Punjab. And lastly, I would like to thank Greg White, who provided me with constant encouragement and support.

I am grateful to Angela Chnapko, editor at Oxford University Press, and Laura Sjoberg and J. Ann Tickner, series editors of Oxford Studies in Gender and International Relations, for seeing the value of a research project that centers the lived experience of minority Sikh women in India. I also want to thank the anonymous readers for their critical insights; thank you for seeing promise in this project. Lastly, I thank Laura Grier for giving permission to use her photograph for the cover of this book.

The ethnographic research that informs this book was conducted with support from the Bhai Gurdas Fellowship, Center for Sikh and Punjab Studies, University of California, Santa Barbara. This book was also supported by Arizona State University's Carstens Family Funded Research Aides, Scholarship, Research and Creative Activities Grant, and School of Social and Behavioral Sciences. Portions of this book are derived in part from articles published in *Politics, Groups, and Identities* and *Space & Polity*: "Situated Citizenship: Understanding Sikh Citizenship through Women's Exclusion," 2014; "Diasporic Researcher: An Autoethnographic Analysis of Gender and Race in Political Science," 2017; and "Gendered Discipline, Gendered Space: An Ethnographic Approach to Gendered Violence in India," 2017.

I would also like to thank my friends and family, whose care and affection sustained me through the writing process. To Raquel Zamora and Rebekah Sterling, thank you for your unfaltering support of me and of my ideas. To Annika Mann, Devorah Manekin, and Risa Toha, thank you for your help in navigating academia and motherhood. To Rashi Majithia and Neeru Jindal, thank you for your unconditional love and friendship. You kept me going when the writing seemed impossible.

My family has provided me with unwavering love. Their confidence in me gives me the strength to dream a little bigger and work a little harder. I thank Jagtar Singh Sodhi (my maternal uncle), Paramjit Kaur Sodhi (my maternal aunt), and their family—Palvi Singh, Upkar Singh, Phulbag Singh Sodhi, and Poonam Kaur Sodhi—for making my research in Punjab possible. Without your help, I am lost. I thank Biji, Sumitra Devi Behl (my paternal grandmother), and Mama, Jass Behl, for teaching me the value of family and community; for demonstrating the depths and power of these bonds; and for giving me the linguistic, cultural, and religious knowledge and sensibility to engage in this ethnographic research. I thank Pitaji, Gurbaksh Singh Behl (my paternal grandfather), for his commitment to education, a commitment that was not limited by gender, and for his embodiment of *chardi kala* (eternal optimism).

I thank my parents, Ashok and Jass Behl, for being my first and true teachers, who taught me about love and equality; about *seva* (service) and submission; about freedom and liberation. Without you I am nothing, I do nothing. I thank my siblings, Esha Behl, Ankit Behl, and Digvijay Singh, for the joy they bring to my life. Without you I am nothing, I do nothing. I thank my life partner, Corey Vuelta, for his generosity, loyalty, and love. Without you I am nothing, I do nothing. I write out of love for my son, Elan Behl Vuelta, and my nieces, Huntleigh Behl, Aria Singh, and Anika Singh. I write for your future; I write to teach you about love and equality; about *seva* and submission; about freedom and liberation. Without you I am nothing, I do nothing.

Politics in Unusual Places

Understanding Gendered Citizenship

and Gendered Violence

POLITICS IN UNUSUAL PLACES: SITUATED CITIZENSHIP AND EXCLUSIONARY INCLUSION

On December 16, 2012, Jyoti Singh,[1] a twenty-three-year-old female physiotherapy student, and her male friend, a twenty-eight-year-old software engineer, were attacked on a bus in Delhi, India.[2] The attack lasted for forty minutes, during which time six men beat the engineer unconscious and gang-raped the female student.[3] In addition to sexually assaulting her with an iron rod, they slapped her in the face, kicked her in the abdomen, and bit her lips, cheeks, and breasts. Ram Singh, one of the assailants, confessed to police that he and the other men burned the victims' clothes, washed the bus, and removed flesh from the seats following the attack (Sharma, Agarwal, and Malhotra 2013). Badri Nath Singh, the victim's father, said of the attack: "They [the perpetrators] literally ate my daughter. There were bite marks all over her" (Sharma 2013). Ultimately, the perpetrators dumped the victims naked and bleeding on the side of the road and attempted to run them over. Jyoti Singh died a few weeks later from massive internal injuries; her friend survived.

On the one hand, Indian democracy has been consistently rated as a successful, consolidated democracy. In addition, Indian democracy has embedded gender equality into its political institutions since the creation of its modern constitution. On the other hand, gendered violence in India has the practical consequence of cutting off women's access to the public spaces required to support that democracy. Jyoti Singh's brutal murder brings a hidden picture of gendered violence—from physical assault to economic and emotional violence—into a very public light (chapters 2 and 3). Despite constitutional guarantees of women's formal equality, Indian women's lived experience reveals a more complicated picture, where experiences of citizenship are plagued with everyday discrimination, exclusion, and violence in the private and public spheres.

This horrific event sparked a national debate within the institutions of Indian government and among its citizens that highlights a tragic contradiction within Indian democracy—one that gravely affects its institutions and ultimately puts its citizens at risk. It begs the question, why do we find pervasive gender-based discrimination, exclusion, and violence in India when the Indian constitution builds an inclusive democracy committed to gender and caste equality? Jyoti Singh's violent murder illustrates the contradictory nature of Indian democracy—the promise of radical equality and the tragic failure to attain this equality. Jyoti Singh's brutal gang rape demonstrates that even though all citizens may be accorded equal standing in the constitution of a liberal democracy, such a legal provision hardly guarantees state protections against discrimination, exclusion, and violence.

The book, *Gendered Citizenship*, argues that conventional understandings of citizenship and democracy cannot adequately explain pervasive gendered violence in both public and private space and instead see it as a bizarre anomaly, insolvable paradox, or intractable problem. Most democratization scholars study gender equality by studying one-dimensional indicators of gender inclusion, such as the number of women in elected national legislatures or gender equality clauses in constitutions. According to Aili Mari Tripp (2013, 514), "This bias in the literature limit[s] a fuller understanding of the relationship between regime type and women's status." Tripp (2013, 514–515) calls for more sophisticated and robust measurements of democratic representation and participation concerned with "gender inequalities across a wide range of outcomes beyond formal representation." I respond to Tripp's call by analyzing multiple dimensions and domains of democratic inclusion and participation.

This book weaves an analysis of the 2012 gang rape and the subsequent political and legal debates with ethnographic data with members of the Sikh community to explain women's unequal experience of democracy in multiple domains—state, civil society, religious community, and home. These two analyses are linked together in a single study because in their linking they call attention to the dangers that lurk in every case of sexual and gender-based violence (SGBV), from its most extreme and horrific expression to the more commonplace repressions of daily life. I by no means seek to flatten the extreme difference between these iterations of SGBV—between the unimaginable and the indignities of a more mundane experience. But I want to highlight the similar logics and perspectives at play along the entirety of the spectrum. I also want to highlight how these logics cause women's lives to be at risk in *all* spheres of life.

At its core, the book sheds light on a paradox in the lived experience of Indian democracy and, in so doing, highlights a serious shortcoming in traditional scholarship. I ask why women's lives are potentially at fatal risk in the everyday sites of public participation and in the private space of the home, when Indian democratic institutions are nominally inclusive in terms of gender equity.[4] Addressing this question reveals a theoretical and methodological blind spot in some political science scholarship—a blind spot that results in the reproduction of gender blindness and the legitimization of gendered violence.[5]

The book proposes *situated citizenship* as a general theoretical and methodological framework to understand the contradictory nature of democracy in any context and then applies this framework to understand uneven experiences of Indian democracy. Theoretically, situated citizenship captures the fact that citizenship is more than a fixed legal status; it is also a situated social relation. Methodologically, situated citizenship requires that as researchers we be situated within local contexts to understand citizenship. Through an analysis of lived reality, situated citizenship highlights how citizens understand and experience the promises of formal equality—moving researchers past the supposed impasse at an institutional level and toward an understanding of the mechanisms by which these contradictions are incorporated in daily life. I characterize the experience of this contradiction as *exclusionary inclusion*, whereby contradictions within all spheres of life, from private belief to the institutions of government, reinforce an uneven and unequal democratic experience, but also potentially renegotiate that unevenness and even challenge it.

Situated citizenship as an approach explains how and why subordinated groups experience, negotiate, and resist exclusionary inclusion in multiple domains. A theory of situated citizenship makes citizens' embodied, lived experience of gender and other intersecting categories of difference central to the analysis, and thus helps explain how and why citizenship has failed its promise of equality. As legal status, situated citizenship requires an analysis of citizens' access to civil, political, and social rights. As an embodied intersectional social relation, situated citizenship enables an analysis of mediating forces, such as relations of power, and asks how these forces affect citizens' standing as members and participants in their communities.

This book responds to an important gap in the citizenship literature. According to Ruth Lister, there is an imbalance between theoretical and empirical work on citizenship. Lister (2007, 58) calls for more empirical studies of the "cultural, social and political practices that constitute lived citizenship for different groups of citizens in different national and spatial contexts." I respond to Lister's call by developing the framework of situated citizenship, which enables empirical analysis of exclusionary inclusion in different contexts, including subnational, national, and transnational.

Exclusionary inclusion refers to a range of practices—legal, institutional, ideological, material, and embodied practices—that cause limited membership in different domains. Exclusionary inclusion allows different entities to minimize their own participation in discrimination and distance themselves from exclusion and violence, while advancing other interests—majority group domination, religious autonomy, minority rights, family values—over equality. Exclusionary inclusion often operates in a reinforcing fashion across different sites, from the public sphere to the private space of the home, and yet these sites are independent of one another. As a result, scholars cannot assume that social relations are experienced uniformly across these different domains. In fact, this is an open empirical question.

While situated citizenship and exclusionary inclusion have implications for studying lived experiences of unequal democracy across a variety of subordinated demographics in different geopolitical locations, this study focuses on gender-based experiences of democratic unevenness in India. Through a situated study of Indian women's lived experience, I demonstrate how the state and formal, legal equality can operate in undemocratic and exclusionary ways. I also show that religious communities can be a surprising resource for women's active citizenship, enabling women to both uphold and resist exclusionary inclusion. Situated citizenship provides a more nuanced and detailed understanding of exclusionary inclusion while also identifying potential sources for challenging it.

Through a situated analysis of citizenship, this book maps how the mechanisms of exclusionary inclusion operate in multiple spheres—state, civil society, religious community, and home—to create women's second-class citizenship.[6] I show how similar gendered norms—such as norms about women's rights and duties and women's religiosity—operate in state-citizen relations, in interpersonal relations, in religious relations, and in kinship relations to limit women's inclusion and participation, to police their behavior and bodies, and to determine their worth and standing. I also show how women negotiate, navigate, and resist exclusionary inclusion in these different domains. A situated analysis of citizenship makes visible the mechanisms of exclusionary inclusion that limit inclusion for some, explains the contradiction between expressed commitment to equality and lived reality of inequality within and between multiple levels of analysis, and asks how these limitations and contradictions impact democratic participation and inclusion for all.

The book contributes to growing literature on the impact of unwritten rules and social norms on public policies and social reforms (Chappell 2014; Raymond et al. 2014; Waylen 2014; Hochstetler and Milkoreit 2014). According to Leigh Raymond and S. Laurel Weldon (2014, 181), "*Informal institutions*, or the sets of 'unwritten' rules . . . frequently cause behavior that is inconsistent with formal laws and policies . . . [yet they] receive relatively little attention from those trying to solve important policy challenges." I address Raymond and Weldon's concerns by turning our attention to informal institutions—in particular gendered norms—to understand the seemingly intractable problem of women's integration into the world's largest democracy and their pervasive experience of discrimination, exclusion, and violence.

Prevailing academic understandings of the relationship between secular state and religious community in India often assume that state-citizen relations are democratic and religious relations are nondemocratic.[7] When it comes to gender, scholars often assume that the liberal democratic state protects women through law as equal citizens, while religious communities subordinate women through traditional practice as unequal members.[8] This book upends these assumptions—this analysis finds that religious spaces and practices can be sites for renegotiating the terms of democratic participation, while secular mechanisms designed to include can be sites for exclusion.

This book takes up the project of analyzing gender relations in different sites to provide detailed evidence that challenges long-standing assumptions about key concepts, such as democratic participation, civil society, religious space, and women's agency. An ethnographic analysis of Sikh women's lived experience of civil society demonstrates that prevailing understandings of civil society as a space of free, voluntary associations do not always hold true. Similarly, detailed ethnographic evidence about Sikh women's experience of religious community demonstrates that established assumptions about religious space as hierarchical and oppressive are not always accurate. Likewise, thick ethnographic description of Sikh women's devotional practices reveals that predominant understandings of religious women as willing participants in their own subordination are not entirely correct.

Democratization scholarship tends to universalize the experience of Western liberal democracies and apply it to the Third World (Rai 1994; Rudolph 2005; Keating 2007, 2011; Das and Randeria 2014). It has been long assumed that the preconditions for establishing a democratic polity are economic development, high rates of literacy, and ethnic and religious homogeneity. Similarly, it has long been assumed that the preconditions for establishing modern citizenship are low levels of premodern forms of affiliation (i.e., religious, kin, and caste groupings), high levels of affiliation with and loyalty to republic (state and nation), and high levels of voluntary association.

In India, none of these conditions were met. Veena Das and Shalini Randeria (2014, 163) assert that the Indian experience reveals the ethnocentrism of Western political theory itself. Similarly, Aya Ikegame (2012) finds that various forms of citizenship have been systematically subjugated by Eurocentric political theory because strong religious, communal, and kinship ties in non-European societies are treated as antithetical to modern citizenship.[9] Christine Keating (2007, 132) argues that Eurocentric modes of theorizing overlook "transformative work being done to recast democracy on more egalitarian and inclusive terms in postcolonial polities."[10] A situated analysis of citizenship makes visible forms of citizenship—in particular religious practices—that remain outside of most theoretical and empirical understandings of citizenship. A situated approach to citizenship also uncovers how some women engage in religious community in unexpected ways to create more egalitarian gender relations. Situated citizenship enables an examination of how the very definitions of civic life are themselves resisted, tested, expanded, and appropriated by citizens on a daily basis as they live.

This study also contributes to a growing literature on women's agency in devotional organizations across faith communities, which adopts an expanded understanding of agency to challenge false dichotomies of devout women as either empowered or subordinated (Mahmood 2005;

Isin and Ustundag 2008; Bilge 2010; Isin 2011; Ikegame 2012; Singh 2015; Banerjee-Patel and Robinson 2017). According to Saba Mahmood (2005, 14), "The normative political subject of poststructuralist feminist theory often remains a liberatory one, whose agency is conceptualized on the binary model of subordination and subversion. In doing so, this scholarship elides dimensions of human action whose ethical and political status does not map onto the logic of repression and resistance." I respond to Mahmood's concerns by focusing attention on interconnected understandings of human and divine agency that operate within multiple meanings of both liberation and submission.

To understand how women's integration into the world's largest democracy and their pervasive experience of gendered violence can coexist, I utilize original data based on extended participant observation, sustained immersion, and in-depth, semi-structured interviews with members of the Sikh community. Sikhs are a minority religious community in India. Followers of the Sikh faith often understand their religious community as a space of gender and caste equality. The Sikh case provides insight into the difficulties of achieving gender equality in the world's most diverse democracy differentiated along gender, caste,[11] class, religious,[12] linguistic, and tribal[13] lines. The Sikh case also illuminates the tensions between state and religious community, between majority and minority religious communities, and between state, community, and gender. Lastly, the Sikh case highlights the contradiction between an ideal of gender equality and the lived experience of inequality, which parallels women's contradictory experience of belonging vis-à-vis the state.[14]

This book uses an interpretive research design and analysis that is more concerned with questions about contextuality and meaning-making than questions about generalizability (Schwartz-Shea and Yanow 2012, 47–48). This type of research design aims to produce research findings that are sufficiently contextualized so that scholars can determine the relevance of specific research questions and findings for other research settings (Schwartz-Shea and Yanow 2012). Similarly, this type of research seeks to adequately contextualize research findings so readers can evaluate the trustworthiness, systematicity, and transparency of the research design and interpretation (Sprague 2005; Hawkesworth 2006a; Schwartz-Shea and Yanow 2012).

While the full range of interpretive methodological approaches can be used to study situated citizenship, this book uses a political ethnographic approach because it requires an awareness of and sensitivity to embodied lived experience, meaning-making processes, and self-reflexivity (chapter 2). Political ethnography relies on immersion to generate detailed evidence and thick description, which can, in turn, open up the possibility of "theoretical vibrancy" and "epistemological innovation" (Schatz 2009) especially as it relates to seemingly insolvable problems. A situated, ethnographic analysis of citizenship explains (1) why it is so difficult to achieve gender equality even when it is constitutionally mandated and protected; and (2) how in the face of exclusionary inclusion some women are able to, albeit in a limited fashion, link the goals of gender equality and minority religious autonomy to create more egalitarian relations and to resist exclusionary inclusion.

Through an interpretive research design, this book explores a continuum of mechanisms used to control women's bodies, to limit their inclusion and participation in democratic society, and to police their behavior in civil society, community, and home. At one end of the spectrum is violent sexual assault and rape. At the other end of the continuum are gendered norms and informal rules that determine who has access to food, healthcare, education, inheritance, and property rights.[15] Violence in the private sphere is inseparable from more visible violence in the public sphere.[16] Both public and private forms of gendered violence[17] are often used to create women's exclusionary inclusion in India.[18] I adopt R. Amy Elman's (2013, 237) definition of gender violence as practices that "represent a violent reproduction of gender that specifically functions to enforce and perpetuate female subordination."[19] This definition enables the study of both public and private forms of violence without adopting fixed or homogenous notions of masculinity and femininity.

Lastly, this study contributes to multiple literatures dedicated to explaining and eradicating the causes and consequences of SGBV in the Indian context. Some scholars approach the issue of SGBV in the

Indian context from a postcolonial framework (Sangari and Vaid 1999a; Subramanian 2014), while others deploy a political economy frame (John 1996; Bhavani et al. 2016). Some researchers address the question of gendered violence in India through a legal framework (Menon 1999, 2004; Baxi, Rai, and Ali 2007; Baxi 2014), while others adopt a caste and communal approach (Sarkar 2001; Das 2007). This study underscores the importance of a contextual cultural-religious approach, which can be used to supplement and extend these other approaches to SGBV in India (chapter 2).

OVERVIEW OF THE BOOK: CONTRADICTIONS OF INDIAN DEMOCRACY AND CITIZENSHIP

The remaining chapters examine women's experiences of democratic unevenness and their negotiation of and resistance against exclusionary inclusion in multiple domains from the intimacy of the home to public political and religious life. Chapter 2 advances a theory and methodology of situated citizenship, which is used in the rest of the book to make visible and intelligible the mechanisms and consequences of exclusionary inclusion.

In developing a framework of situated citizenship, I review democratization and legal studies literatures, identify the major limitations of these literatures, and explain how a theory of situated citizenship overcomes these limitations. Many of these scholars assume that citizenship rights are determined by constitutions and statutes; however, this assumption overlooks the fact that often the localized practices of exclusionary inclusion determine whether women can exercise their formal rights. These scholars also point to the existence of certain laws and statutes to argue that Indian women are full citizens; however, they do not ask if these laws construct the very gendered oppression they seek to eradicate. Lastly, these scholars emphasize the number of women in elected national legislatures or gender equality clauses in constitutions as evidence of gender equality; however, they do not ask if these institutions and laws are experienced in a biased way. What remains unexamined is the extent to which formal, legal approaches effectively achieve gender equality, engender behavioral and attitudinal changes, and empower women.[20]

I argue that institutional indicators and formal rights fail to tell the full story—and hide more than they show because through nominal female inclusion these formal institutions often render the mechanisms of exclusionary inclusion invisible. I develop a theory and methodology of situated citizenship to explain how uneven and unequal experiences of citizenship are created, maintained, and challenged in the private and public spheres through concrete face-to-face social practices often compounded by intersecting categories like gender, caste, class, religion, and nation (Glenn 2002, 2; Hawkesworth 2013, 49).

In developing situated citizenship as a theory, I draw on feminist and critical scholars of citizenship, who often follow the Marshallian conception of citizenship because it is a normative vision about equality *and* an analytic tool for determining inequality (Siim 2013, 758; see also Marshall 1950, 1964; Hall and Held 1990; Held 1991; Lister 1997; Yuval-Davis 1997; Yuval-Davis and Werbner 1999; Glenn 2000, 2002, 2011; Lister et al. 2007; Roy 2014). This literature helps to advance a theory of situated citizenship because it challenges "the assumption that once suffrage was achieved for women, blacks, and other minorities, all citizens became automatically equal subjects" (Yuval-Davis and Werbner 1999, 4). Rather than assuming equality as a starting point, these scholars ask whether citizenship is experienced unequally depending on intersecting forms of difference—age, class, race, ethnicity, religion, gender, sexuality, and (dis)ability (Yuval-Davis and Werbner 1999, 4–5).

In advancing situated citizenship as a methodological approach, I draw on feminist and critical approaches to methodology in political science that expand existing methods to include interpretivist approaches, which understand data as cogenerated by the researcher and researched, and knowledge production as political (Shehata 2006; Tickner 2006; Hawkesworth 2006a, 2006b; Pachirat 2009; Schatz 2009; Schwartz-Shea and Yanow 2012; Ackerly and True 2010, 2013; Campbell 2015). This literature is useful in developing a methodology that is sensitive to the lived experience of power relations because it challenges positivist claims of neutrality and calls for political science to study itself and its research communities as sites of politics (Hawkesworth 2006b; Weldon 2013; Ackerly 2018).

The remaining chapters investigate the gap between expressed commitment to equality and a lived experience of inequality in all spheres of life, from private beliefs, attitudes, and behaviors to the institutions of government. Chapter 3 focuses attention on women's uneven and unequal experience of the Indian state through an examination of the political and legal debates surrounding the 2012 gang rape. Chapter 3 examines both the progressive political opening and the retrenchment of patriarchal norms following Jyoti Singh's murder, and argues that this opening and retrenchment are emblematic of the Indian state's radical promise of equality and its horrific failure to achieve this equality. An analysis of politicians' responses demonstrates how gendered norms—women's religiosity and women's rights and duties—operate in the state, and how these norms are used to exclude women in the name of inclusion. This analysis highlights the difficulty of eradicating gendered violence through legal reform, demonstrates the unpredictability of the political process, and shows how gendered norms operate in the public sphere to undermine and frustrate progressive change.

Chapter 3 also situates the 2012 gang rape in larger debates about the current tensions between state, religious community, and gender. In doing so, chapter 3 draws on and contributes to feminist and critical legal studies, which challenges the assumption that legal institutions and standards can arbitrate social power in an objective, impartial, and neutral fashion. This scholarship sheds light on the contradictory nature of Indian democracy because it demonstrates how legal institutions construct social power, and how the law is constitutive of power relations (West 1988; King 1988; Crenshaw 1989, 1991; Williams 1991; Harris 1990; Matsuda ([1988] 1992; Merry 2000; Gomez 2000, 2008; Menon 1999, 2004; Cramer 2005). I rely on feminist and critical legal scholars to raise the following questions: Can scholars and activists turn to law as a liberatory strategy, when it creates and maintains women's unequal citizenship? Can researchers, activists, and political actors eradicate gendered violence given the uneven and contradictory nature of the Indian state and law?

Chapters 4 and 5 uses semi-structured, in-depth interviews with members of the Sikh community to analyze exclusionary inclusion in civil society, religious community, and home. Through an ethnographic examination of interpersonal, religious, and kinship relations, I map how one minority religious community in India both upholds exclusionary inclusion and resists it. These chapters are animated by the following questions: How are dimensions such as religion, ethnicity, caste, and gender implicated in structuring the material circumstances of women's lives and their experience of citizenship? Are Sikh women full members of their communities? Do Sikh women have the capacity—the civil, political, and social resources—to effectively exercise their citizenship rights? Do Sikh women experience civil society, religious community, or home as a site of liberatory politics? These questions matter because they are central to understanding and transforming exclusionary inclusion. The goal of these chapters is to demonstrate how gender intersects with other identity categories to determine who is most vulnerable to violence, who has actual power to be active as citizens, and who can command democratic participation and action.

Chapters 4 utilizes interview and participant observation data to focus on Sikh women's lived experience of exclusionary inclusion in civil society and the home. Chapter 4 demonstrates how research participants construct the category of woman in relation to home and marriage, and how they naturalize exclusionary inclusion through the following unwritten and informal rules: (1) women's rights and duties, (2) public policies, (3) women's religiosity, (4) women's purity, and (5) women as perpetual outsiders. A majority of research participants understand gender equality and religious autonomy as competing goals, which makes it more difficult to achieve equality. The ethnographic data reveals that Sikh women do not experience civil society as an uncoerced space of voluntary associational life, and they do not experience the home as a place of safety, security, and respect. Rather they experience exclusionary inclusion in both these spaces.

Chapter 5 uses interview and participant observation data to demonstrate how Sikh women both uphold and resist exclusionary inclusion in religious community. Sikh women often struggle to escape contradictory and conflicting gendered norms—women's religiosity, women's rights and duties, and women's purity—that essentialize women as inferior, polluted, and suspect. Yet, for some women, membership in Sukhmani Seva Societies (devotional organizations) is an unexpected resource for active citizenship, where they sometimes reinforce but sometimes also resist socially prescribed gender roles and discriminatory gender norms that cause their unequal belonging. These women enact their citizenship rights through their religious affiliation. A situated analysis of women's participation in Sukhmani Seva Societies opens up the possibility for understanding acts of devotion as acts of citizenship, thus questioning long-standing assumptions about religious relations as inherently undemocratic. Sikh women active in devotional organizations can teach scholars and activists something about the current impasse in the debate regarding state, religious community, and gender in India. Without explicitly engaging this debate, Sikh women envision and enact more egalitarian interpersonal and community relations through their devotional practices, which understand gender equality and minority rights as coexisting and human and divine agency as interdependent. Their experience suggests that religious practices can be understood as a form of active citizenship that can potentially challenge exclusionary inclusion and negotiate between state, minority community, and gender in new ways.

In the concluding chapter, I return to the 2012 gang rape and murder of Jyoti Singh. I reanalyze this horrific incident in light of the research findings and discuss the implications of my analysis for the study of gender equality, citizenship, and democracy in India and beyond. I also critically reflect on my positionality as diasporic researcher, with attention to the ways participants and I coconstruct the data, and to the ways my own blind spots impact the research process. Lastly, I ask if political science as a discipline is willing to listen to new forms of knowledge production.

Situated Citizenship

An Intersectional and Embodied

Approach to Citizenship

Indian democracy constitutionally protects gender equality and has been led by influential women across all spheres of government. Despite these facts, Indian women are some of the most marginalized in the world.[1] On the one hand, Indian democracy has been regularly regarded as a democratic success. On the other hand, gendered violence in India undermines women's access to the very public spaces needed to sustain that democracy.

Indian democracy is a model of democratic transition and consolidation[2]—India has adopted and maintained universal adult franchise, has had mostly free and fair elections, and has viable political parties across the ideological spectrum, as well as a vibrant press, a professional military, and an independent judiciary. When it comes to gender, India is again a model of democratic transition and consolidation—India has had a female prime minister, a female president, multiple female leaders of prominent political parties, many strong female state leaders, a reservation system guaranteeing women 33 percent of village council seats, a growing female representation in the Lok Sabha (lower house of parliament), and a growing female voter turnout.

Indian law explicitly codifies women's formal equality. Indian women won constitutional parity—including enfranchisement—prior to ratification of the Indian constitution.[3] India is a constitutional parliamentary democracy, with written Fundamental Rights containing extensive equality provisions: Article 14 guarantees equality; Article 15 restricts the state from sex-based discrimination; Article 16 guarantees equal opportunity; Article 39.d guarantees equal pay for equal work; and Article 19 guarantees freedom of speech and expression, freedom of association, freedom of travel, freedom of residence, and freedom to form labor unions.[4] The Indian constitution protects gender equality, while also retaining a plural system of personal law that protects cultural differences but perpetuates gender-based inequalities.[5]

Data on violence against women reveals a hidden picture.[6] A 2012 household survey by UN Women found that 95 percent of women and girls feel unsafe in public spaces in the capital city, Delhi.[7] The survey also found that 51 percent of men self-reported perpetrating violence against women and girls in public spaces.[8] An analysis of nationwide data on crimes against women reveals that on average, every hour in India two women are raped, four are kidnapped, one dies in a dowry-related dispute, four are molested, one is sexually harassed, and eleven experience an act of cruelty by their husband (Indian National Crime Records Bureau).[9] While Jyoti Singh's gang rape and murder received a great deal of national and international attention, assaults like it occur routinely.[10] Gender-based violence is disturbingly commonplace, and conviction for such crimes is low.[11] Indian women's lack of safety, both experienced and perceived, undermines their ability to access public spaces necessary for democratic participation.[12]

Institutional indicators and formal laws fail to tell the full story about Indian women's paradoxical experience of democracy. In response to this failure, I develop a theory and methodology of situated citizenship to explain how contradictory experiences of citizenship are navigated, negotiated, and resisted in the private and public spheres. In developing this theory, I draw on feminist and critical scholars of citizenship who call for more empirical scholarship that examines how citizens and social groups understand and negotiate their rights, membership, and belonging in different sites (Siim 2013, 760; see also Lister 2007). In advancing situated citizenship as methodology, I draw on interpretivist scholars who call for more empirical research that captures situated meaning, which can be used to challenge shared assumptions, rethink accepted beliefs, interrogate faulty arguments, and reframe research questions (Hawkesworth 2005, 144; see also Schwartz-Shea and Yanow 2012).

Situated citizenship highlights how citizens understand and experience the promises of formal equality in all spheres of life. Situated citizenship requires an intersectional and embodied approach to citizenship, which moves us beyond questions of formal equality, and asks how mediating forces, such as norms and informal rules, impact citizens' capacity to enact their citizenship rights and to take democratic action. As legal status, situated citizenship requires an analysis of citizens' access to civil, political, and social rights. As an embodied intersectional social relation, situated citizenship asks how power relations affect citizens' standing as members and participants in their communities. As a methodological approach, situated citizenship requires sensitivity to embodied lived experience, meaning-making processes, and self-reflexivity, which, in turn, can make visible uneven experiences of democratic citizenship.

In reviewing conventional approaches to democracy and law, I show how these approaches tend to maintain gender blindness and perpetuate gendered violence. Research dedicated to proving that Indian democracy is consolidated and that Indian women are full citizens often neglects evidence of everyday forms of gendered violence even though feminist scholars have provided the theoretical and methodological tools to make sense of this violence. This theoretical and methodological failure results largely from a narrow definition of politics as the study of formal governmental institutions, political elites, and electoral politics. While research committed to using law as tool to solve social problems often assumes that the purpose of law is unquestionably correct and overlooks the impact of these laws in people's lives. This theoretical mistake arises primarily from a failure to incorporate decades of feminist and critical scholarship that challenges liberal understandings of law as neutral and objective.

According to Mary Hawkesworth (2005, 152), "The replication of gender bias in political science impedes the discipline's ability to explain the political world . . . [and] reproduces and legitimates male power and gender injustice." This chapter provides insight into the difficulty of understanding gendered violence in political science and achieving gender equality within democratic societies. A situated approach to citizenship highlights why it is so difficult to make relations—state-citizen relations (chapter 3) and citizen-citizen relations (chapters 4 and 5)—more democratic and inclusive in the face of exclusionary inclusion. A situated framework to citizenship demonstrates why, as Shirin Rai (1994, 218) states, "the non-availability of a 'democratic' public space makes it very difficult for women to oppose the regime that enforces their exclusion."

The experience of the 2012 gang rape victim underscores that lives are at stake in this analysis. The way we define politics, the way we categorize democracy, and the way we conceptualize citizenship matters because we can define these concepts to either illuminate or overlook gendered citizenship and gendered violence. By situating citizenship, political science can bring everyday practices back into examination, it can widen the vision of the political, and it can make gender and gendered violence central to its analysis.

In the following section, I review traditional approaches to democracy and law and demonstrate the limitations of these literatures. I argue that a theory of situated citizenship is necessary because it overcomes the gender blindness of traditional approaches and provides a better understanding of uneven experiences of democratic citizenship. Next, I describe the primary theoretical and methodological dimensions of situated citizenship and explain how they expand on feminist and critical approaches to citizenship and feminist and interpretivist approaches to methodologies, respectively.

GENDER BLINDNESS IN TRADITIONAL APPROACHES TO DEMOCRACY AND LAW

To shed light on women's lived experience of Indian democracy, I initially turned to the mainstream democratization and legal studies literature.

Given the relationship between democracy, law, and equality, one would expect these literatures to provide insight on women's unequal experience of democracy. However, in reviewing these literatures I found them to be part of the problem, as they reproduce and legitimize gender blindness by failing to incorporate decades of feminist and critical scholarship.[13]

For decades, gender and politics scholars have demonstrated that democratization scholarship is gender-blind and have provided the tools necessary to overcome this blindness (Beer 2009; Caraway 2004; Paxton 2000; Tripp 2013; Waylen 2007). This is a recognized and prevailing problem in the field of comparative politics, yet democratization scholars continue to omit gender in their definitions, measurements, and operationalization of democracy.[14] This gender blindness within mainstream democratization literature is a result of narrow definitions of democracy, one-dimensional measurements of women's democratic inclusion and participation, and highly flawed operationalization of democracy.[15] This continued omission of women biases our understanding of the origins, causes, and history of democracy, and ignores gendered violence in democratic societies.[16]

Scholarship on democratization conceives of democracy in such a way as to write women out of the very definition.[17] Even when democratization scholars use definitions of democracy that incorporate women's suffrage, they often operationalize these definitions in ways that exclude women.[18] The so-called objective indexes and indicators used to measure and operationalize democracy are themselves biased because they exclude women's citizenship rights. How can researchers rely on such measures to make sense of women's democratic inclusion, if these very measures conclude that countries are democratic when women are not permitted to vote? How can scholars and activists rely on such measures to understand women's experience of exclusionary inclusion, when they fail to acknowledge something as fundamental as women's formal equality?

Some gender and politics scholars respond to the gender blindness of traditional democratization scholarship by adopting more robust and sophisticated indicators of gender inclusion, participation, and equality, rather than one-dimensional indicators (Tripp 2013). Still others respond by expanding the study of democracy beyond formal institutions of democracy to include public sphere and civil society (Htun and Weldon 2010; Walsh 2012). I respond by advancing a theory of situated citizenship because it can make visible, and perhaps actionable, the gendered nature of political science as a discipline and women's contradictory experience of democratic citizenship.

For decades, critical legal scholars,[19] from feminist sociolegal scholars to critical race theorists and intersectionality scholars, have demonstrated that law is neither objective nor neutral, but rather is constitutive of power relations (West 1988; King 1988; Crenshaw 1989, 1991; Williams 1991; Harris 1990; Matsuda ([1988] 1992; Merry 2000; Gomez 2000, 2008; Menon 1999, 2004; Cramer 2005). This is an acknowledged and long-standing critique in the field of legal studies, yet legal scholars continue to ignore the role of law in constructing gendered and raced hierarchies. This gender and race blindness within mainstream legal studies is primarily caused by a faulty assumption that legal institutions mediate social power in an objective, impartial, and neutral fashion.[20] Critical legal scholars argue that context matters because legal standards are embedded in larger power structures (West 1988, 765).

Critical legal scholars demonstrate the contradictory nature of law as a potential source of equal rights for women and racialized minorities.[21] These scholars acknowledge the transformative value of legal rights for disempowered people in multiple social movements across the globe, for example, civil rights movements (Bell 1980; Delgado 1984), feminist movements (Agnes 1996; Menon 1999, 2004), battered women's movements (Merry [1988] 1992), and disability movements (Schweik 2009, 2011). Yet these scholars also call for a more critical engagement with law as an emancipatory strategy.

According to Nivedita Menon (1999, 278), "We need to recognize . . . that social movements may have reached the limits of the discourse of rights and of 'justice' as a metanarrative."[22] Similarly, Crenshaw (1995, xxiv) states, "We [critical scholars of color] wanted to acknowledge the centrality of rights discourse even as we recognized that the use of rights language was not without risks." How can scholars rely on legal equality as an indicator of women's democratic inclusion, if the very laws that enshrine women's equality discriminate against them? How can activists see law as a means to end women's oppression, when it creates women's second-class citizenship? How can researchers and activists turn to law as an emancipatory strategy, when it maintains women's experience of exclusionary inclusion?

I, like the many feminist and critical legal scholars who have come before me, cannot resolve the contradiction between law and lived experience, between law and justice. However, I can advance a theory of situated citizenship, which enables scholars to map this contradiction, and locate potential sources to challenge it.

SITUATED CITIZENSHIP: AN INTERSECTIONAL AND EMBODIED THEORETICAL FRAMEWORK

In developing a general theory of situated citizenship, I draw on feminist and critical scholars, who often combine liberal and republican traditions of citizenship by bringing together a liberal formulation of free and equal rights-bearing citizens with a republican emphasis on active political participation and civic engagement.[23] These scholars define citizenship as membership in a political community, where one enjoys rights and duties, and where one actively participates.[24] Liberal citizenship emphasizes formal legal status, and protects individual rights against the state and others.[25] This model of citizenship is often described as a "thin conception of citizenship-as-status" (Kymlicka and Norman 1994, 354–355). In contrast, republican conceptions of citizenship emphasize active participation in deliberation and decision-making toward a common good.[26] The republican model is often referred to as a "thick conception of citizenship-as-activity" (Kymlicka and Norman 1994, 354). It must be noted, however, that feminist and critical scholars bring these two traditions together while problematizing the meaning of the "common good," challenging universal approaches to citizenship, and deconstructing the separation between public and private.

Feminist and critical scholarship on citizenship often uses T. H. Marshall's approach as a key reference for contemporary analysis of citizenship.[27] Marshall defines citizenship as full membership in a community in terms of three sets of rights—civil, political, and social (Marshall 1950, 1964). Theoretically, situated citizenship builds on a Marshallian conception because it allows for a double focus: citizenship as a failed promise of equality and citizenship as a normative vision for equality.

Another advantage of Marshall's definition is that it links citizenship to membership in a community rather than the state, which enables an analysis of citizenship as legal status and social relation.[28] A theory of situated citizenship expands on scholarship that envisions citizenship as legal status and social relation because such a conception enables an examination of activities, practices, and experiences beyond the state and beyond the "politics of electoral competition" (Hanchard 2006, 27).[29]

Feminist and critical scholars also expand the Marshallian conception by focusing on what Marshall overlooked. Scholars criticize Marshall's framework for its Eurocentric and male bias. In response to these biases, some scholars shift focus to the rights of cultural and religious minorities (Kymlicka 1995; Tully 1995; Parekh 2000). Others explore the exclusion of racialized groups from the full enjoyment of rights (Roediger 1991; Forbath 1999; Mills 1999; Lopez 2006). Still others examine the exclusion of women focusing on the gendered nature of citizenship (Okin 1979; Pateman 1988, 1989; Smith 1989; Lister 1997a, 1997b; Siim 2000). These scholars ask: do citizens enjoy the capacity to enact their citizenship rights given existing power relations (Hall and Held 1990; Held 1991)?

Feminist scholars also criticize liberal and republican models of citizenship for their shared assumption of a separation between the public and private spheres, which gives primacy to the private sphere, protects it from outside interference, and hides oppression within the family (Okin 1979; Pateman 1988, 1989; Lister 1997a).[30] Feminist scholars argue that the so-called neutral distinction between the public and private is a political construction that reflects historical and social power differences, and is constantly contested and negotiated. A situated approach to citizenship builds on scholarship that interrogates the public/private divide by showing how the mechanisms of exclusionary inclusion operate within all spheres of life, from the intimacy of the home to the institutions of government, to reinforce an unequal democratic experience.

These scholars also criticize a universal model of citizenship and develop alternative theories of citizenship that encompass difference (Lister 2007, 52). The goal of this scholarship is to recognize and respond to difference while avoiding assimilation or exclusion from the political community (Yuval-Davis 2006b, 207). Feminist critiques of universalism come primarily in two forms. First, these scholars reveal the male citizen lying beneath false claims to universalism and make visible the female noncitizen who remains outside (Okin 1979; Pateman 1988, 1989; Smith 1989; Lister 1997a, 1997b). Second, these scholars demonstrate the false universalism of the category of woman assumed to be white, middle-class, and heterosexual (Combahee River Collective [1977] 1997; hooks 1981, 1994; Anzaldúa and Moraga 1981; Feminist Review 1984; Collins 1986, 1989, 1990; Anzaldúa 1987). A situated model of citizenship avoids the problems of universalism by insisting on an intersectional approach,[31] which requires sensitivity to multiple, coconstituted, and interlocking differences and subordinations.[32]

Lastly, feminists and critical citizenship scholars demonstrate how citizenship has "failed its promise of equality" (Lister et al. 2007, 10). These scholars challenge the assumption that suffrage guarantees equality (Yuval-Davis and Werbner 1999, 4). Often scholars do so by focusing on lived citizenship (Lister 1997b; Yuval-Davis 1997; Yuval-Davis and Werbner 1999; Glenn 2000, 2002, 2011; Siim 2000, 2013; Lister et al. 2007). Lived citizenship refers to "the meaning that citizenship actually has in people's lives and the ways in which people's social and cultural backgrounds and material circumstances affect their lives as citizens" (Hall and Williamson 1999, 2). Lived citizenship requires that researchers "take into account local practices that recognize or deny standing to certain groups and individuals irrespective of their formal standing under constitutional provisions or statutory law" (Glenn 2011, 2–3). Lived citizenship captures how individuals navigate the three dimensions of citizenship in their daily lives: rights, belonging, and participation (Lister et al. 2007, 168). As a result, lived citizenship refocuses researchers' methodological attention to multiple spheres of experience. Situated citizenship draws on lived citizenship to make central the daily lived experience of citizens as they negotiate civil, political, and social rights, and as they navigate inclusion, membership, and belonging in multiple spheres.

Situated citizenship, however, is distinct from lived citizenship because it provides concrete tools for potentially transforming meanings and understandings of citizenship. Situated citizenship extends the work of lived citizenship because it can shift the way we think about citizenship itself. Situated citizenship is open to the observation that the categories and spaces in which citizenship and the civic can be practiced are continually being expanded, contested, and appropriated in sometimes unusual places and unexpected ways. Situated citizenship also extends lived citizenship by highlighting often overlooked theoretical questions by holding the tension between abstract normative theory and lived experience at the center of any analysis. Such an approach opens up the possibility of creating new forms of "situated knowledge . . . marked by place, time, and circumstance" (Rudolph 2005, 12), which can, in turn, force a rethinking of taken-for-granted concepts.[33] Lastly, situated citizenship provides concrete methodological tools to better understand multiple experiences of citizenship. Situated citizenship relies on interpretive research design and methodology to open the possibility of collecting new kinds of empirical data (from archival to ethnographic) that often remain outside the focus of researchers. These new forms of data can potentially take seriously local, contextual knowledge and make visible often overlooked forms of political life.

I advance a situated approach to citizenship because this approach (1) expands the focus beyond the state to directly examine social relations in multiple domains to determine who is included and to what extent; (2) makes gender central to political analysis, while being sensitive to embodied intersections between gender, religion, and other identity categories;[34] and (3) expands the focus of political science beyond abstract formal equality to relations of power, which make visible exclusionary inclusion.

Beyond Formal, Legal Equality

Political scientists often assume that citizenship is a fixed legal status, and once this legal status is achieved, then all citizens uniformly enjoy equality (Glenn 2011).[35] Such conceptions of citizenship assume that citizenship status is linear and progressive and overlook the fluidity of citizenship, which is determined, in part, through complex and contradictory, daily-lived experience.[36] In this analysis, I move beyond notions of citizenship as narrow formal legal status and adopt a definition of citizenship as legal status *and* embodied intersectional social relation. Doing so focuses attention on (1) the gap between rights in theory and rights in practice; (2) practices, behaviors, and opinions that differ from espoused commitment to equality; (3) law as constitutive of unequal citizenship; and (4) exclusionary ways of defining membership and belonging in civil society, religious community, and home. Such an analysis does not assume equality as the starting point, but rather asks how lived experiences, material circumstances, and embodied difference affect the lives of supposedly equal citizens in liberal democracies.

Beyond Narrow Definitions of the Political

Political scientists often adopt a narrow definition of politics focused on state and government (Hanchard 2006; Hawkesworth 2006b; Weldon 2013). As a result, political science as a discipline primarily studies formal governmental institutions, political elites, and electoral politics. A narrow definition of politics assumes that power operates only in the formal institutional spaces of government and fails to consider how power operates beyond the formal realm. Jyoti Singh's gang rape and murder demonstrates that relying on objective institutional measures and formal law while neglecting women's lived experience makes researchers horrifically blind to the ways institutional indicators and legal statutes do not align with lived realities, produces erroneous classifications when it comes to questions of democracy and citizenship, and fails to fully analyze the relationship between citizenship and gendered violence. I adopt an expanded definition of the political, a definition that enables an analysis of exclusionary practices in often overlooked sites of politics, including civil society, religious community, and home.[37]

Beyond Western-centric Notions of Citizenship

Theoretically and empirically, certain forms of citizenship have been and continue to be systematically ignored by Eurocentric political theorists, who often characterize strong religious, communal, and kinship ties as antithetical to modern citizenship (Ikegame 2012). In response, some scholars call for an investigation of "citizenship after orientalism" (Isin 2002, 2012), which is committed to deorientalizing and decolonizing citizenship. These scholars "undo, uncover, and reinvent" (Isin 2012) citizenship to provide a deeper understanding of citizenship's history and future (Chakrabarty 2000; Mignolo 2006; Isin and Ustundag 2008; Isin 2008, 2011; Ikegame 2012). According to Aya Ikegame (2012, 690–691), "The image of 'citizenship after orientalism' . . . [is] a possible form of citizenship which emerged out of dialogues with colonial modernity yet still remains outside of our theoretical understanding of citizenship." Situated citizenship contributes to this literature by making visible forms of citizenship— in particular religious practices—that remain outside our theoretical and empirical understanding of citizenship in liberal democracies.

SITUATED CITIZENSHIP: AN EMBODIED AND SELF-REFLEXIVE METHODOLOGICAL FRAMEWORK

In advancing situated citizenship as a general methodological approach, I draw on feminist and critical approaches to methods and methodology in political science that expand existing methods to include interpretivist approaches, such as interview, ethnography, discourse analysis, archival research, field research, participatory action research, and community-based research (Shehata 2006; Tickner 2006; Hawkesworth 2006a, 2006b; Pachirat 2009, 2018; Schatz 2009; Schwartz-Shea and Yanow 2012; Ackerly and True 2010, 2013; Campbell 2015). These scholars also advocate for more creative interpretive methods and methodology, such as narrative, storytelling, autoethnography, biography, personal testimony, playwriting and performing, poetry, and other artistic endeavors (Schwartz-Shea and Yanow 2012; Dhamoon 2013; Isoke 2018).

Most research strategies in political science draw upon positivist conceptions of the scientific method (Somit and Tanenhaus 1967; Greenstein and Polsby 1975; Finifter 1983; Seidelman and Harpham 1985; King, Keohane, and Verba 1994; Geddes 2003). According to positivist methodologies, political scientists can capture objective reality because adherence to rigid procedures—in the context of systematic experiments, logical deductions, and statistical analysis—controls for the researchers' subjectivity (Hawkesworth 2006b, 29). As a result, positivist methodological approaches claim to be "neutral" and deny any political dimension to scientific inquiry. Positivist political scientists evaluate research studies based on the standards of validity, reliability, and replicability. Interpretivist methods, however, do not meet these evaluative standards, and therefore, most political scientists characterize interpretive approaches as unscientific, biased, and invalid (Shehata 2006; Pachirat 2009; Schwartz-Shea and Yanow 2012).

In contrast, feminist and critical scholars challenge positivist claims of neutrality and argue that data is cogenerated and knowledge production itself is political (Harding 1986; Twine and Warren 2000; Brown et al. 2003; Hawkesworth 2006a, 2006b; Tickner 2006; Nagar and Geiger 2007; Bonilla-Silva and Zuberi 2008; Schwartz-Shea and Yanow 2012; Ackerly and True 2010, 2013). This scholarship also calls for critical reflexivity, attentive "(1) to unequal power relations, (2) to relationships, (3) to boundaries of inclusion-exclusion and forms of marginalization, and (4) to situating the researcher in the research process" (Ackerly and True 2013, 136).

In developing situated citizenship as a theoretical and methodological approach, I also draw from and contribute to a growing field of study called "grounded normative political theory" that recognizes that research is itself part of a system of power, and therefore scholars are required to reveal and theorize "the arrangements of power and powerlessness in the struggle and in the *inquiry*" (Ackerly 2018, 141 and 149).[38]

Situated citizenship as an interpretive methodological approach can capture lived experience and meaning-making processes through embodied research, which generates insights about exclusionary inclusion that would otherwise be overlooked.[39] While situated citizenship can use the full range of interpretive methodologies to study unequal experiences of democracy in any context, this study relies primarily on ethnographic[40] (chapters 4 and 5) and autoethnographic (chapter 6) methods to understand exclusionary inclusion within the Sikh community in India and within political science as a discipline.

Political ethnography's insistence that the embodied experience of the ethnographer and research participants be part of the research process can bring attention to informal institutions, unwritten rules, and gendered and raced norms, which are in tension with formal institutions and laws. The thick description and detailed evidence of political ethnography can reveal the unknown and unpredicted, which has the potential to upend long-standing assumptions. Zenzele Isoke (2018, 152) asks, "Isn't it the role of the ethnographer to discern meaning through the shock of the Event, through her own brokenness?" She (2018, 158) also asks, isn't it her role "to lean into her own brokenness . . . as a break away from traditional epistemes" to make visible "the profundity of our paradoxical existences"? As an ethnographer, I both witnessed and experience(d) the very gendered norms that cause exclusionary inclusion, I both witnessed and experience(d) the profound paradox of democratic equality (chapter 6). Accordingly, ethnography enables the researcher to "weigh those made-in-the-academy concepts and techniques against the situated, specific, and beautifully complex lived experiences of the actual social worlds" (Pachirat 2012). Also, by requiring an awareness of embodied lived experience, meaning-making processes, and self-reflexivity, political ethnography can demonstrate that "the politics of embodiment is epistemically, morally, and substantively relevant to academic research" (Hawkesworth 2013, 52).

Political ethnography is a methodological approach that relies on immersion or participant observation; according to Schatz, it is "a *sensibility* that goes beyond face-to-face contact . . . to glean the meanings that . . . people . . . attribute to their social and political reality" (Schatz 2009, 5; see also Bayard de Volo and Schatz 2004; Shehata 2006; Pachirat 2009, 2018; Forrest 2017). Through close, person-to-person contact, ethnography conveys realities with an unmatched level of precision, which often call into question prevailing understandings of the political world (Fenno 1978; Scott 1985; Cohn 1987; Soss 2002; Pachirat 2011; Campbell 2014; Brodkin 2017).

Ethnographic knowledge is shaped "by the shifting, contextual, and relational contours of the researcher's social *identity* and her social situatedness or *positionality* (in terms of gender, race, class, sexuality, and other axes of social difference), with respect to her subjects" (Nagar and Geiger 2007, 267; see also Shehata 2006; Pachirat 2009; Schwartz-Shea and Yanow 2012).[41] According to Samer Shehata (2006, 246), "In ethnography, the ethnographer's self becomes a conduit of research and primary vehicle of knowledge production." As such, ethnography requires that the researcher critically reflect on her role in every aspect of the research process, which, in turn, makes the research process more transparent and increases the trustworthiness of knowledge claims (Schwartz-Shea 2006, 102; Schwartz-Shea and Yanow 2012, 104).

Political ethnography asks what and who gets left out of traditional definitions of politics, argues that the definition of what is political is an issue of power, and often explodes traditional definitions of the political. According to Timothy Pachirat (2009, 144), "Political ethnography is *political* precisely because of its unique potential to both illuminate politics and challenge established conceptions of its boundaries, [and because] fieldwork inevitably locates the ethnographer within networks of power." Similarly, M. David Forrest (2017, 111) finds that "the public value of political ethnography lies in its exceptional ability to advance political science . . . as a project aimed at disrupting forms of power." The benefits of such an approach, according to Edward Schatz (2009, 4), are that it "helps ensure an empirically sound, theoretically vibrant, epistemologically in-novatively, and normatively grounded study of politics."[42]

I advocate for an ethnographic approach to citizenship because it enables an analysis of power relations in often overlooked sites of politics—from private belief and behaviors in the home to fieldwork, "deskwork" and "textwork" in the research process (Schwartz-Shea and Yanow 2012, 101). I use the detailed evidence of political ethnography to weigh the ideal of democratic equality against the complicated and contradictory lived expe-rience of this ideal. In doing so, I make visible and legible the mechanisms of exclusionary inclusion.

Methodology

The ethnographic research that informs this book was carried out over multiple trips to Punjab, India, between 2000 and 2010 (Behl 2009, 2010, 2012, 2014, 2017a). During this time, I engaged in extended participant ob-servation, sustained immersion, and in-depth, semi-structured interviews. I lived with informants, was embedded in local communities, and was pre-sent for and participated in major life moments within local communities, such as weddings, births, deaths, and celebrations. I also attended political rallies, campaign events, community organized meetings, and religious ac-tivities within local communities. Lastly, I observed interactions between politicians and constituents, and interactions among citizens in multiple settings. I conducted two sets of semi-structured, in-depth interviews based on snowball sampling—one during winter 2003–2004 with thirty female politicians in Mohali district, and the other during spring 2009 with forty research participants, men and women, in Mohali and Amritsar districts.[43] I use the term research *participant*, rather than research *subject* because this term acknowledges participants' agency in the research pro-cess (Schwartz-Shea and Yanow 2012; Ackerly and True 2010, 2013).

I selected interview participants through "chain referral": (1) I relied on my informants to make initial contact with research participants; and (2) participants whom I interviewed suggested others in their networks.

I knew my informants through familial relations prior to my fieldwork experience. The informant from Mohali district was active with the Akali Dal party and the informant from Amritsar district was active in the Congress party. Both informants used their political, personal, occupational, and religious networks to introduce me to participants. Through this sampling method, I interviewed Sikhs of varying socioeconomic backgrounds, degrees of religious observance, and political affiliation.

The interviews lasted from 30 to 120 minutes and were conducted in Punjabi. I conducted "relational interviews" that rely on dynamic dialogue between researcher and interviewee to uncover how people construct meaning (Fujji 2018, 3).[44] I asked participants general questions about gender.[45] I also asked participants about their expectations and opinions on religion and gender, women's role inside and outside the home, personal law, dowry deaths, and sex ratio. I used broad, open-ended questions to allow participants to define equality, woman, and discrimination on their own terms. By doing so, I gathered cogenerated data on gender roles, and the degree to which individuals approved of these gender roles. I transcribed each interview, and then developed a coding scheme to interpret participants' answers. I use the language of interpretation to draw attention to the fact that as a researcher I did not simply observe patterns in the data.

In 2009, in total, I interviewed twenty-one men and nineteen women. The oldest respondent was seventy-one, and the youngest was twenty-one. Participants varied in educational levels: seven were uneducated/illiterate, eleven completed some primary education (K–ninth classes), ten completed some secondary education (tenth–twelfth classes), and twelve completed some higher education (beyond twelfth class). Participants also varied based on religiosity: twelve identified as *amritdhari*, twenty-two identified as *kesdhari*, and six identified as *sehajdhari* (most traditionally religious to least traditionally religious).[46] Participants varied based on political affiliation as well: ten identified with Indian National Congress, fifteen identified with Shiromani Akali Dal, nine identified as independent, and six declined to state. In addition, participants varied based on caste: nine identified as Khatri, fourteen as Jat, and seventeen as scheduled/backward caste. In the book, I often use the category of upper caste to refer to Jats and Khatris, and use the category of scheduled caste (SC) to refer to former untouchables or Dalits and backward castes identified by the Indian state as deserving special benefits to ameliorate casteism. To ensure participants' confidentiality, I use pseudonyms throughout the book.

My positionality as a Sikh woman undoubtedly shaped the interview data (see chapter 6). My prior knowledge, Punjabi language mastery, race/ethnicity, religion, and familial contacts enabled me to gain access in a way that other researchers may not. For example, I had multiyear relationships with my informants previous to my academic field experience. I lived with my informants and relied on their networks and reputation in local communities. However, I simultaneously encountered disadvantages because of my personal background. My positionality generated and blocked access to research situations. As Peregrine Schwartz-Shea and Dvora Yanow (2012, 67) argue, none of these demographic factors "is an automatic, universal key to open all doors: each one can play either or both ways, sometimes opening doors, sometimes shutting them."

It should be noted that my small-*n*, nonrandom sample is not intended to be representative. I do not make any claims about producing generalizable or representative knowledge. Instead, I argue that these interviews are illustrative of exclusionary inclusion. In particular, I find a contingent alignment between spiritual and political liberation for some women in the Sikh community. This particular finding could perhaps be unique to the Sikh case. This is an open empirical question that requires further research. Situated citizenship as a framework can be used to conduct future research about varied understandings of liberation beyond the Sikh community. This framework can also be used to understand exclusionary inclusion in any community.

CONCLUSION

In this chapter, I review conventional approaches to democracy and law to explain why a theory of situated citizenship overcomes gender blindness and provides a better understanding of exclusionary inclusion. I adopt a situated approach to citizenship because it insists on an intersectional analysis, adopts a more expanded definition of the political, and moves beyond formal, legal equality. I also argue that ethnography is the best way to study situated citizenship because it emphasizes lived experience, meaning-making processes, and self-reflexivity. Situated citizenship avoids the trap of gender blindness because it makes visible, and perhaps actionable, the horrific reality that some citizens experience democracy differently; some citizens are more vulnerable to violence.

In the following chapters, I explain how citizens understand and experience the promises of formal equality in multiple domains. Chapter 3 focuses attention on the state through an analysis of the political debates following Jyoti Singh's brutal murder. I select this moment because it exemplifies a political opening—a promise of gender equality—and a subsequent political closure—a promise failed.

Unequal Citizenship

Secular State, Religious Community, and Gender

When asked about the treatment of Sikhs in India, Hardeep Kaur Bedi, a fifty-five-year-old Khatri woman, answers:

> We don't need anyone to give us anything; we Sikhs have our own separate law. We love our religion; we have our own way of dress; we have our own identity; we have created our own social norms of how we interact and interrelate. We have created all of this on our own. Our *qaum* [nation] is just like this; no one needs to give us anything. We don't need anything. Our gurus have given us so much, and they continue to watch over us, and we actually do better on our own, as the lions that we are.

Bedi's response raises interesting questions about the relationship between state and minority religious community, especially as it relates to the tensions between secular law and religious norms, between national and subnational loyalties, and between individual rights and community solidarity. However, it is also important to note that the category of gender is absent in Bedi's discussion. Gender is often the invisible or overlooked category in academic and popular understandings of the relationship between an Indian secular state and (majority and minority) religious communities.

Historically and currently, Indian women's bodies often become the site of struggle between the state and religious communities, yet women themselves are absent from these debates.[1] I focus attention on the tensions between the state and religious communities to illustrate how women's bodies, rights, and mobility are bound up in these tensions. I also highlight women's uneven and unequal experience of the Indian state through an examination of the political and legal debates surrounding the 2012 gang rape. I examine the progressive political opening and the retrenchment of patriarchal norms following Jyoti Singh's murder, and argue that this opening and closure are emblematic of the Indian state's radical promise of equality and its horrific failure to achieve this equality. An analysis of politicians' responses demonstrates how gendered norms—women's religiosity and women's rights and duties—operate in the state, and how these norms are used to exclude women in the name of inclusion. This analysis highlights the difficulty of eradicating gendered violence through legal reform, demonstrates the unpredictability of the political process, and shows how gendered norms operate in the public sphere to undermine and frustrate progressive change.

I rely on feminist scholars to outline the current impasse between state, religious community, and gender (Sunder Rajan 2003; Menon 2004; Keating 2011). In light of this impasse, I raise the following questions: Can scholars and activists turn to law as a liberatory strategy, when it creates and maintains women's unequal citizenship? Can researchers and activists eradicate gendered violence given the uneven and contradictory nature of the Indian state and law? This analysis dispels the idea that legal institutions are objective and neutral in their arbitration of social power and provides insight on the difficulty of achieving gender parity through the state. In response, I use an ethnographic analysis of the Sikh community to move beyond the realm of state and law, I turn our attention to civil society, religious community, and home, and I ask to what extent these sites might be potential sources for more egalitarian gender relations (chapters 4 and 5).

In the following sections, I demonstrate how women experience the state, citizenship, and law as contradictory and uneven. Next, I turn our attention to the 2012 gang rape because this horrific murder galvanized the country and opened up the possibility of radical legal reform to combat SGBV. However, this opening was met by a reinstitution of patriarchal laws, which illustrates the contradictory nature of Indian democracy. Lastly, I turn our attention to the Sikh minority community and examine exclusionary and inclusionary dynamics within this community.

SECULAR STATE, RELIGIOUS COMMUNITY, AND GENDER

This section outlines the tensions between an ostensibly secular Indian state and majority and minority religious communities, and explains how these tensions manifest in the highly divisive political and intellectual debate regarding a uniform civil code (UCC) as a replacement for personal law (Agnes 1996, 68; Sunder Rajan 2003, 147). I highlight how women—their bodies, rights, and mobility—are entangled in these tensions between the cultural rights of minority groups and equal rights for women,[2] between majority group domination and minority group autonomy, between national cohesion and religious freedom. I also focus attention on women's differential experience of the state and law within this context.

Indian women's experience of the state has been mixed. On the one hand, the Indian state promises women's equality through its constitutional guarantees and its legislative interventions on behalf of women.[3] On the other hand, the Indian state has failed women, as is evidenced in nearly every indicator of women's status: sex ratio, literacy rates, employment, infant mortality, and life expectancy.[4] Women experience the Indian state as contradictory. The very Indian state that has miserably failed women also protects women's equality, intervenes on their behalf, and responds to their concerns, albeit in limited and complicated ways.

Nivedita Menon (1999b, 18) finds that "the relationship of women's organizations with the state is often contradictory—on the one hand, the state is seen as the primary agent perpetuating oppression of women, and on the other, the state is treated as the agent of change and potential protector of powerless sections of society."[5] The Third World state, according to Shirin Rai and Geraldine Lievesley (1996, 1), is best understood "as an uneven and fractured terrain with dangers as well as resources for women's movements." Given the uneven nature of the Indian state, it is a meaningful yet unpredictable site for achieving women's empowerment.

Citizenship is also experienced by Indian women as contradictory. An analysis of Indian citizenship requires that we acknowledge both the inclusive and exclusive nature of the Indian constitution. On the one hand, it contains extensive equality provisions that fully integrate women and guarantee gender parity.[6] On the other hand, it retains a plural system of personal law, a legacy of British rule, that actively subordinates women.[7] Majority Hindu and minority Muslim, Christian, and Parsi communities have their own personal laws, while other religious groups, including Sikh, Buddhist, and Jain, are governed by Hindu personal law. All Indians are governed by personal law because no citizen may opt out of a religious identity, and therefore no one is free from personal law. Personal law secures cultural autonomy for communities, but limits women's rights because control over women's bodies is a primary way of expressing cultural autonomy.

Personal law impacts nearly all aspects of a woman's life: "It determines her status at birth; her capacity to own, inherit, and manage property; her freedom to work, marry, divorce, and remarry; and her relationship with her children" (Htun and Weldon 2011, 145). Menon (1999b, 10) argues that "all [personal laws] discriminate against women. . . . In all cases, women become the symbols of community identity and any attempt to change the position of women gets perceived as an assault on the community." As a result, the issue of personal law divides women on multiple fronts—between their respective religious communities, between civil rights and minority rights, and between gender equality and minority claims for recognition.

Notwithstanding discriminatory personal law, Indian citizenship is far more inclusive than Western models, as the constitution explicitly includes and integrates women, illiterates, scheduled castes, and other marginalized groups, while most Western models failed to do so and only integrated these groups after long protracted struggles. According to

Christine Keating (2007, 135), the Indian constitution explicitly challenges Western liberal democratic forms of exclusions by "lifting formal restrictions to public political life for women and minorities and explicitly recognizing the need to address questions of gender and minority group equality as part of the foundation of the new polity." Unlike women, indigenous, and minority populations in the West, Indian women and minority groups won constitutional parity, including enfranchisement and cultural group recognition, prior to ratification of the Indian constitution (Trivedi 2003, 184).

Indian citizenship, however, has multiple complications. According to Keating (2007, 131), the constitution "sanctioned discriminatory personal laws that maintained women's subordination in the family in order to secure fraternal acquiescence to centralized rule." Similarly, Flavia Agnes (1996, 74) argues, "The freedom to regulate the 'personal' or 'domestic' sphere was offered [by colonial rulers] as a carrot to native men (and in the present context, to the minorities) so that there is an easy acceptance of political rule in public life." This creates a contradictory situation where women are full and equal citizens in India, yet they are governed by patriarchic personal laws that undermine their equality. This contradiction arose because "fraternal masculinist" interests were privileged over gender equality (Keating 2007, 2011).

All groups in India, however, do not experience cultural autonomy uniformly. Keating (2007, 141; 2011, 5) argues that by formally barring discrimination based on race, ethnicity, or religion, the framers of the constitution laid the groundwork for a multicultural democracy. However, by abolishing measures that would have ensured minority group political strength (such as reserved seats and communal electorates), the framers created a model of multicultural democracy that cemented majority group domination and consolidated Hindu political hegemony in national politics (Keating 2007, 141; 2011, 5).[8] Similarly, Agana Chatterji, Shashi Buluswar, and Mallika Kaur (2015, 21–22) find that "majoritarian democracy" in India is incompatible with pluralism and equality.

Religious minorities in India enjoy full and equal citizenship, yet they lack the political strength to challenge Hindu domination. Personal law represents one of the few tools available to minority religious communities to maintain their religious autonomy. As a result, the stakes for maintaining (or gaining) separate personal law are extremely high. The minority Sikh community has its own code of conduct (Rahit Maryada), but not its own personal law. Rather, Sikhs are incorporated under the Hindu personal law. There is a long history of Sikhs agitating for a separate Sikh identity, separate personal law, and, at times, a separate Sikh nation-state. A segment of the Sikh community understands itself as a separate nation (*qaum*) with its own religion, language, and territory.[9] These claims for autonomy are evident in 1898 in Kahn Singh Nabha's influential text *Hum Hindu Nahin* [We are not Hindus] and in the 1970s and 1980s in Sant Jarnail Singh Bhindranwale's popular preaching.

Often Sikh women find themselves torn between their commitments to their religious minority community and their individual rights as liberal, secular citizens. Sikh women feel a strong solidarity with their religious community, which was violently persecuted by the Mughal empire and British Raj, and is presently persecuted by a so-called secular Indian state that maintains Hindu religious and political hegemony. Sikh women's experience can be understood as part of a larger constitutional contradiction between women's rights as individual citizens and rights of religious communities as collective units of a liberal democracy.

Uniform Civil Code

At the time of independence, the framers of the constitution advocated for a UCC because it would ensure legal uniformity and national cohesion in the face of religious difference (Agnes 1996; Menon 1999b; Sunder Rajan 2003). However, the UCC was never fully adopted, and personal laws were maintained to minimize communal conflict.[10] Religious minority communities oppose a UCC because it threatens their religious freedom and religious identity. Minority communities also fear that the UCC will be used as a veiled way of imposing Hindu law for all citizens. Communitarians also oppose a UCC because of their support for a plural, decentralized polity in which religious communities enjoy autonomy (Sunder Rajan 2003, 150). In contrast, majority Hindu nationalists support a UCC because, as Sunder Rajan (2003, 149) notes, they see it as a way of securing Hindu law and Hindu hegemony. Liberal secularists also support a UCC because they see it as way of achieving equality, uniformity, and cohesion, yet they are highly aware of the vulnerable position of minorities (Sunder Rajan 2003, 150).

The debate regarding UCC brings together some very unlikely allies. According to Flavia Agnes (1996, 68), two improbable partners—women's organizations and Hindu fundamentalists—advocate for a UCC. This convergence of interests puts Indian feminists "in an unenviable position of juxtaposing women's rights and minority rights" (Agnes 1996, 69). Similarly, Sunder Rajan (2003, 150) highlights unlikely convergences "between the liberal/left and the Hindu right favoring a UCC, for instance, and between secular communitarians and fundamentalist representatives of minority communities that oppose it."

There is very little consensus among feminist scholars and activists when it comes to the UCC debate. According to Menon (1999a) and Sunder Rajan (2003), the one thing feminists agree on is the fact that *all* personal laws of *every* religious group are discriminatory against women. On most other issues, feminists find themselves conflicted and torn.[11] Some advocate for a compulsory UCC, while others promote an optional egalitarian civil code; some advocate for reform initiated from within religious communities, while others support internal reforms plus state-sponsored legislative reform.[12]

Indian civil and criminal law also discriminates against Indian women. According to Ratna Kapur (2007, 133), Indian civil law essentializes women as "caretakers, mothers and wives in need of protection." Similarly, Veena Das (2007, 26) finds that the Indian state defines women as sexual and reproductive beings, not as citizens.[13] Such assumptions result in laws that curtail women's rights and endorse violence against women. For example, rape is illegal in India, but there are exceptions to what counts as rape. Following the 2012 fatal assault of Jyoti Singh, the definition of what constitutes rape was widened to include any nonconsensual penetration of the mouth, anus, urethra, or vagina with the penis or other object, and nonconsensual oral sex. However, marital rape is still not considered a crime in India (Human Rights Watch 2012; Lodhia 2015; Sachdev 2016). Similarly, in India public policies on domestic violence often protect family and family values, not victims of domestic violence. According to Kapur (2007, 133), proposed reforms to domestic violence policies "sanctioned the right of men to beat their wives with reasonable cause, which included instances where a wife made a grab for her husband's property." Indian law—personal, civil, and criminal—is not neutral, objective, or impartial; rather it actively creates women's inequality. In the next section, I demonstrate how a recent amendment to Indian criminal law supposedly designed to protect women actually marginalizes them.

GENDER AND CITIZENSHIP IN THE 2012 GANG RAPE CONTEXT

The unprecedented media attention and massive protests following the 2012 fatal gang rape of Jyoti Singh created a political opening for gender equality. Protests, demonstrations, and candlelight vigils were held throughout India. Many Indians—men and women of all ages, socioeconomic levels, educational levels, religious backgrounds, and ideological backgrounds—related with and saw themselves in Jyoti Singh.[14] The brutal incident galvanized citizens to come together and fight against SGBV. This moment exemplifies a promise of gender equality culminating with the progressive Justice Verma Committee (JVC) report, which argues that sexual assault is a symptom of a larger problem—patriarchy in India.[15] Yet this opening was followed by a political closure—the adoption of the Criminal Law (Amendment) Act 2013, popularly referred to as the 2013 Anti-Rape Law, which ignored the JVC report and enshrined discrimination.[16]

In response to countrywide public outcry, the government established the JVC to propose possible amendments to Indian criminal law with the goal of providing quicker trials and enhanced punishments for perpetrators of sexual assault and extreme violence against women. The JVC (Verma,

Seth, and Subramanium 2013, i) completed its review of Indian criminal law in thirty days and prescribed sweeping changes to rectify "the failure of governance to provide a safe and dignified environment for the women of India." The JVC (2013, i) understood the political potential of the moment: "Let us hope that this tragedy [Jyoti Singh's murder] would occasion better governance, with the State taking all necessary measures to ensure a safe environment for the women in the country, thus preventing the recurrence of such sexual violence." Hope is a central theme in the opening pages of the JVC report.

The Verma committee expresses "fervent hope" (2013, iv) for Jyoti Singh, for the citizens of the country, for civil society, and for the Indian government. The committee (2013, iv) "hopes that the . . . constitutional promise of gender justice . . . will soon be realized . . . [which] would be the real tribute to the memory of the victim of gang rape." The committee (2013, 22–23) also "hopes to have successfully addressed the concerns of the people, and done justice to the widespread protests across the country." The JVC also hopes that "the three arms of governance, viz, the executive, the judiciary and the legislature, will take the recommendations made herein to their logical conclusion" (2013, 16) and "move collectively towards a culture of equality and mutual respect" (2013, 22–23). The committee reflected the hope of many Indian citizens, who saw Jyoti Singh's tragic murder as a call for actualizing the constitutional promise of gender equality.

2012 Gang Rape

Massive segments of the Indian population sympathized with Jyoti Singh because they viewed her as a middle-class girl who was assaulted by criminal, poor, lower-caste, migrant men.[17] Many Indians read the rape as an assault against the urban middle class, and therefore they saw themselves in Jyoti Singh's horrific experience even though Singh's life story was far more complicated. Many understood the 2012 gang rape by creating two categories of citizen: *deserving* citizen, characterized as urban, middle class, educated, and upper caste, and *nondeserving* citizens, characterized as rural, poor, illiterate, and lower caste. This categorization of deserving and nondeserving citizens differentiated by gender, caste, class, geographic location, and education creates a false opposition, in which the nondeserving actively attacks the citizenship rights of the deserving. Such a characterization subverts the promise of equality for all and creates the possibility of protecting the rights of some citizens against the rights of others. This case demonstrates that even those citizens who are moved by Jyoti Singh's brutal rape, who are galvanized to protest and demonstrate for gender equality, often reproduce intersecting forms of subordination.

Jyoti Singh was the first in her family to pursue a professional career.[18] Her parents migrated to New Delhi from a poor village in Uttar Pradesh before her birth. In November 2008, she enrolled in a physiotherapy program at Sai Institute of Paramedical and Allied Sciences in Dehradun, India. To afford her tuition, her father, an airport worker, sold most of his land in his village, borrowed money from family members, and worked sixteen-hour shifts handling luggage at the airport, while Jyoti Singh worked nights at a call center helping Canadians with their mortgage issues. In October 2012, Jyoti returned to Delhi to look for a volunteer internship, a requirement of her physiotherapy program. Jyoti Singh and her family were far from middle class; her family poured all of their resources into Jyoti's education in the hopes of achieving middle-class status.

Nevertheless, Jyoti's brutal murder was read as part of a larger narrative of an urban, middle-class lifestyle under assault by the criminal, lower-caste, and rural poor. According to Kabeer (2015):

> The six men in question came from one of the squalid slum neighbourhoods of Delhi. . . . They fit the face of the image of the rapist "monster" in the public imagination in a way that rapists in the police force, the army and the upper castes do not . . . the scale of the response we are seeing is a manifestation of class outrage.

Crimes against middle-class, upper-caste women mobilize the middle class and upper caste, whereas gendered violence against minority, scheduled- and backward-caste, and tribal women is ignored.[19] Rape and other forms of gendered violence, such as mutilation, burning, and stripping and parading women, are common tools used to maintain gender, caste, class, and religious oppression in India, yet they do not lead to media attention and citizen protests. Minority, lower-caste, and lower-class women experience uneven and unequal protection in multiple spheres of life. Rarely do these women's experience of gendered violence result in state-sponsored commissions and reports and civil society protest and demonstrations. And when they do, it is because their experience is used to pursue other interests—majority group domination, middle-class interests, religious autonomy, family values, national security, national unity, and so on.

What is overlooked in most national and international media reports is the fact that Singh's family and her assailants come from similar backgrounds. The rapists, like Singh's father, migrated from rural villages, belonged to the backward Kurmi caste, and earned approximately the same amount of money per month (Roychowdhury 2013). Even though Singh and her assailants shared many similarities, media accounts portray Singh as a liberal and upwardly mobile individual and her rapists as criminal, lower-caste, and rural poor. As Roychowdhury (2013, 284) explains, "Media stories imagined that if only, somehow, this unsavory sector of the Indian population could be controlled, or disappeared, India would be safe for women. Until that promised day, the presence of rural, working-class, slum-dwellers in the city would continue to pose a threat, curtailing the new Indian woman's—and metonymically, the new India's—progress." This characterization of an urban, middle-class woman under assault opens up the possibility of protecting the rights of some *deserving* citizens (urban, professional, and middle-class) at the expense of *nondeserving* citizens (rural, illiterate, lower-class and lower-caste).[20]

Justice Verma Committee Report

The 2012 gang rape, even if momentarily, galvanized a large segment of Indians against SGBV and created an opening for challenging gender injustice. This political opening is most apparent in the JVC report, which was widely described as a landmark document (Kale 2013). The JVC's progressive intervention for gender justice is manifested in how its members define the problem, conceptualize key ideas, delineate the stakeholders,[21] understand the law, and propose comprehensive remedies. The JVC report (Verma, Seth, and Subramanium 2013, 6–7) asks: how can constitutionally guaranteed freedoms be transformed into real freedoms that enable women to fulfill "their potential as individual citizens under India's liberal and democratic framework?" The report (2013, 10) finds that Indian women have suffered substantially in multiple realms, including bodily safety, mental well-being, economic and political empowerment, and self-esteem/self-autonomy because "de facto equality guaranteed by the Constitution has not become a reality for them."

The JVC report (2013, 13) explains the gap between constitutional equality and women's lived experience as state failure: "The Indian State has failed to look at this issue [gender equality] in a substantive manner . . . all organs of the State have, in varying degrees, failed to fulfil the promise of equality in favour of women." The JVC (2013, 6) also finds that law alone is not sufficient for ameliorating women's subordination: "The most perfect laws also would remain ineffective without . . . the human agency for implementing the laws, namely, the law enforcement agencies . . . supported by the complementary role of civil society." The report understands law as embedded in social, political, and religious context, and therefore, law must also be accompanied by societal change. The committee (2013, iv) argues, "Attitudinal changes to correct the aberration of gender bias have to be brought about in the institutions of governance . . . and in civil society."

The report (2013, 8) also adopts a comprehensive understanding of equality that moves beyond formal legal equality:

It is not enough that women occupy a few symbolic political positions to evidence true empowerment of women in this country. In the view of this Committee, the ethos of empowerment of women does not limit itself to political equality, but also extends, in equal terms, to social, educational, and economic equality.

To achieve this broad understanding of equality, the JVC proposes a separate bill of rights for women, which would define certain practices—
including cultural, social, political, religious, and customary norms—as
patriarchal and as impairments on women's agency, dignity, and equality.
The proposed bill of rights would also protect women's right "to express
and experience complete sexual autonomy" (2013, 429).

The report also calls for an expansion of what counts as actionable violence under the law to include marital rape, acid attacks, stalking, sexual
harassment, and trafficking. In addition, the report calls for an expansion
of whose bodies are eligible for the state's protection by abandoning the
marital rape exemption, challenging the Armed Forces Special Provisions
Act (AFSPA), and expanding gender justice beyond women to include
protection of rights of all sexual and gender identities, including lesbian,
gay, bisexual, transgender, and intersexual persons (2013, 41).

The JVC is an example of the inclusionary potential of the state. This
is an instance in which the Indian state identifies *itself* as complicit in
creating and maintaining gender-based inequality, discrimination, and
violence, and proposes radical changes to current Indian law in an effort
to transform gender relations and eradicate gendered violence. The committee intervenes in a way that opens up the possibility for a more democratic and egalitarian form of membership and belonging.

Despite the radical nature of the JVC report, Indian politicians, who
claimed to be acting on the JVC recommendations, adopted the 2013
Anti-Rape Law, which endorses and legitimizes gendered violence by
incorporating only some of the JVC's recommendations. For example,
the Anti-Rape Law expands the definition of rape, increases penalties for
sexual assault, bars the use of a victim's past sexual history in determining
consent, and makes gender-insensitive police and hospital authorities
more accountable. In large part, however, the Anti-Rape Law dilutes and
ignores the JVC's recommendations in several ways: it retains the ex-
ception to marital rape, does not amend the AFSPA so that soldiers can
be prosecuted in civil courts, and fails to extend protections to lesbian,
gay, bisexual, transgender, and intersexual citizens.[22] The Anti-Rape Law
demonstrates the uneven nature of the Indian state, which simultaneously

creates a political opening for gender equality and enacts a dangerous law that privileges men and promotes patriarchy.

Indian politicians responded to the political opening created by the 2012 gang rape by adopting regressive legislative measures. Politicians adopted women's issues to promote their own sexist agenda in which women are simply the objects of the debate. Furthermore, far from securing women's equal access and right to public spaces, these politicians restrict and police women's freedom of association, travel, and mobility in the name of their safety. Certain politicians claim that women provoke SGBV and deserve to be assaulted because they exit the home at the wrong time of day, in the wrong kind of clothing, with the wrong kind of man, and with un-Hindu, un-Hindustani thoughts. Some politicians use legal reform to privilege patriarchal family values, to limit women's access to and mobility in public space, and to actively endorse gendered violence.

According to feminist activist Kavita Krishnan, secretary of the All India Progressive Women's Association, the 2013 antirape legislation purports to be parliament's tribute to Jyoti Singh, but "Far from being a momentous and historic blow to patriarchy . . . the occasion only served to remind us what kind of patriarchal reaction we're up against" (Bhalla 2013). The public and state response following the 2012 gang rape astonished Indian feminists because, all of a sudden, SGBV was on the public agenda, men were standing alongside women questioning sexual violence, and the JVC committee responded with an unprecedented state response acknowledging the state's and communities' responsibility in perpetuating SGBV (Kabeer 2015). However, this momentary political opening was exploited by politicians to push legislation that largely legalizes, endorses, and condones SGBV. The promise of gender equality remained unrealized; the radical political opening was met with a patriarchal political closure.

2013 Anti-Rape Law

Following the brutal attack on Jyoti Singh, some parliamentary discourse used gendered violence as a resource to advance patriarchal interests in the name of women's inclusion. In contrast, the JVC used gendered violence to open up radical questions about gender equality and gendered power relations. Also, some members of parliament and state elected officials shifted blame and responsibility for rape onto the victim by adopting the gendered norms, including women's rights and duties and women's religiosity,[23] whereas, the JVC commission (Verma, Seth, and Subramanium 2013, 11) calls out these very politicians for blaming Jyoti Singh "for having facilitated the rape by her own behaviour." In the following sections, I highlight the responses of some politicians to suggest that gendered norms used to justify exclusionary inclusion in civil society, religious community, and home also operate in parliamentary debate and shape the unpredictability of the debate in the public sphere. It should be noted that this is not intended to be a comprehensive or representative analysis of parliamentary debate.

WOMEN'S RIGHTS AND DUTIES

Some politicians focused on women's rights and duties as wives and mothers when defending the marital rape exemption in the 2013 Anti-Rape Law. These politicians argued that marital rape posed a threat to the institution of marriage. For example, Sumitra Mahajan, from the right-wing Bharatiya Janata Party, explained her support for the marital rape exemption by claiming: "It will destroy Indian families. Things like these should be sorted out within the family or by counseling. There is no need for a law" (Bhalla 2013). By declaring that there is no need for a law, some politicians demonstrate that they do not see women as equal, rights-bearing citizens who deserve state protection from fellow citizens, including their husbands. Rather, these politicians privilege patriarchal family values over gender equality.

Mohan Bhagwat, chief of the right-wing Rashtriya Swayamsevak Sangh (RSS), argues that women should restrict themselves to "household chores" to avoid rape.[24] Bhagwat explains, "A husband and wife are bound by a contract which says 'you (woman) look after the household chores and satisfy me, I (man) will take care of your needs and will protect you'" (Bhatt 2013). According to this logic, women are responsible for their rape because women fail to fully sexually satisfy their husbands and obediently complete their duties as wife and mother bound to marriage and home.

In the debate over the 2013 Anti-Rape Law, some politicians defined women not as equal rights-bearing citizens, but as wives and mothers restricted to home and marriage who do not enjoy equal protection under the law. This results in criminal law that maintains gender inequality and endorses gendered violence because it governs by privileging men, legalizing marital rape, and promoting patriarchal family structures and values. The dilution of the JVC report and passage of the 2013 Anti-Rape Law normalized SGBV by legalizing, condoning, and legitimizing marital rape.

WOMEN'S RELIGIOSITY

Some politicians, like Babulal Gaur, the home minister of Madhya Pradesh, explain SGBV by questioning the victim's religiosity: "Women in south India are comparatively less prone to sexual assault because of their religious nature and their urge to wear full clothes" (Dutta 2014). Vibha Rao, the chairperson of a state women's commission, claimed that women are "equally responsible" for the violence committed against them, stating, "Women influenced by Western culture . . . send wrong signals through their dress and behavior and men often take the cue from those signals" (Bagchi 2013). Other politicians, like Mamata Banjerjee, chief minister of West Bengal, argue that rapes occur because of the decline of purdah (gender-based segregation or seclusion, including veiling): "Rapes are happening because men and women are interacting too freely" (Kabeer 2015). Still others called for a return to purdah as a way to safeguard women from sexual predators. For example, politicians called for segregating school buses, banning skirts, and making overcoats mandatory for girls' school uniforms (Bosco 2013).

Some Indian politicians suggest that Indian women who reject Hindu religiosity deserve to be raped and assaulted; women who refuse modest Hindustani attire and adopt shameless Western attire deserve to be raped and assaulted. Indian politicians often claim that the problem of gendered violence exists elsewhere—in other communities, in other cultures—and therefore a return to Hindu religion and Hindustani culture is required. It is important to note that these politicians make a clear distinction between Hindustan, characterized as rural, traditional, and free from sex crimes, and India, characterized as urban, westernized, and full of sex crimes (Bhatt 2013).

Indian politicians often blame victims of sexual assault by claiming that they are equally responsible for gendered violence because they are not sufficiently religious. Such explanations of SGBV demonstrate that Indian politicians do not see women as equal, rights-bearing citizens; rather they understand women's belonging, membership, and protection as contingent upon their commitment to Hindu religion and Hindustani culture. Through an analysis of political debate surrounding the Anti-Rape Law, we see how politicians' sexist and misogynist views lead to the adoption of a law that fails to fully protect Indian women.

An examination of the 2012 gang rape and the subsequent political and legal debates demonstrates that radical political openings do not easily translate into progressive political change. Often there are changes at the margin, while gender equality remains unrealized, and the momentary political opening is followed by a political closure. This analysis underscores the unpredictability and difficulty of achieving gender justice in the public sphere through legal reform in a liberal democracy. Given this difficulty, I examine if other spheres of life—civil society, religious community, and home—might be potential sources for more egalitarian social relations.

MOVING BEYOND THE INDIAN STATE AND LAW

Many feminist scholars highlight the gap between law on the books and law as experienced by Indian women (Agnes 1992; Menon 1999a; Kapur and Cossman 1999; Sunder Rajan 2003). Flavia Agnes (1992, WS19) states, "If oppression could be tackled by passing laws, then the decade of the 1980s would be adjudged a golden period for Indian women." Likewise, Ratna Kapur and Brenda Cossman (1999, 197) find that "notwithstanding formal guarantees of equality, Indian women's lives continue to be characterized by pervasive discrimination and substantive inequality." How do scholars and activists achieve women's democratic inclusion if legal remedies create the very gender inequality they seek to eradicate? How do we advance gender equality if the law and legal professionals are themselves discriminatory? How do we secure a future for women that is free from the fear of violence given the uneven nature of the state and law? Do we abandon law as a possible liberatory strategy for women?

For some feminist theorists, law alone is not a viable option. Many feminist scholars argue that "independent" and "impartial" legal systems and legal professionals are discriminatory towards women, and therefore not fully effective (Baxi 1982). Others scholars, like Menon (1999a, 262–263), argue that "attempts to transform power relations through law . . . resediment these relations and . . . reassert dominant values." Menon (1999a, 288) responds by underscoring the uneven nature of law: "In deconstructing legal discourse . . . we can recognize the extent to which engagement with the law continues to be inevitable and sometimes fruitful, but also in what ways such an engagement can run counter to our emancipatory vision." For Menon, law cannot be a "subversive site," however, it can be useful in a limited fashion (Menon 1999a, 286).[25]

Given this reality, feminist scholars call for scholarly examinations that move beyond the state and law as potential sites of liberatory politics. Rai (1996, 6) calls for an examination of "women's political activities which include not only opposition but negotiation, not only struggle but also strategic bargaining in spaces that are intersections of the private and the public spheres." Similarly, Sunder Rajan (2003, 147) locates women as " 'national subjects' in relation to, but also beyond, the state and the religion-based community that the UCC debates implicitly regard as providing the only two alternative resources and identities for the female Indian citizen." Likewise, Keating (2011, 106–107) identifies "egalitarian relations on the interpersonal [and] group . . . levels" as a possible source for "an egalitarian pluralism in which gender equity and religious and cultural autonomy are linked goals." All three scholars call on us to move past the state to examine social relations in other domains to determine if they are possible sites for reshaping gender relations in India. I respond to this call by examining both the exclusionary and inclusionary possibilities within civil society, religious community, and home.

These scholars also call on us to question and rethink existing categories of analysis.[26] Menon (2004, 179) states that "feminist politics has [come] to the difficult recognition that 'women' do not simply exist as a category that is available for feminist mobilization." Consequently, Menon (2004, 20–21) suggests that "the creation of 'women' as subject should be understood to be the *goal* of feminist politics, not its starting point." The scholarly task is to take the category of woman, differentiated based on religion, caste, class, nation, and sexuality, as the subject of empirical study. The goal is to explain how and when women come together given these differences, rather than assuming that the category of woman exists a priori, shares a common interest and identity, and can be used as part of our analytic toolkit (Roy 1994; Brubaker 2004; Lee 2008; Beltran 2010).

I respond to these calls by using an ethnographic analysis to open up the category of religion-based community. I ask if religious community is a potential site of liberatory politics for Sikh women. In answering this question, I demonstrate that religious community is not always experienced by women as wholly oppressive. But rather religious community can, albeit in a limited fashion, provide women with the resources to envision and enact gender equity and religious autonomy as paired goals. I also respond to these calls by using an ethnographic analysis to question and rethink the category of woman. I show how Sikh women come to identify as Sikh. I demonstrate how Sikh women are split apart by caste and class differences, and how they overcome caste and class. I map how Sikh men and women define the category of woman so that it limits women to the space of home and marriage. I also map how some women navigate such definitions to gain access to public religious space and civil society.

MINORITY SIKH COMMUNITY

The Sikh community is a minority religious community representing 2 percent of the Indian population, rooted in Punjab, with members throughout India and the world.[27] It is the fifth-largest organized religion, with approximately thirty million Sikhs. The Sikh community regards the guru period—from the birth of the first guru, Guru Nanak in 1469, to the death of the tenth guru, Guru Gobind Singh in 1708—as the golden years of its history. The Guru Granth (guru in book form) provides continuity between the ten historical gurus and Vahiguru (Eternal Guru) and serves as the highest religious authority within the Sikh community.

The radical nature of Sikhism can be seen in multiple institutions and practices, which function to democratize religious space. However, this democratization is incomplete, as women and lower-caste Sikhs have yet to achieve equal status. From the inception of the Sikh faith, the goal for Sikhs has been to apply Sikh teachings in their daily lives by embracing a disciplined worldliness committed to the divine Name (Vahiguru) and human equality. Sikhism espouses a radical equality through its institutions, scripture, and embodied practices.[28] Sikhism grants women and untouchables unprecedented direct access to scripture and *gurdwara* (Sikh temple) without the mediation of male clerics or a priestly caste.[29] Sikhism also envisions and expresses the divine Name, Vahiguru, as the "Formless Infinite" with no gender and no caste.[30] Lastly, Sikhism rejects gender- and caste-based pollution and challenges gender- and caste-based segregation.

Sikh embodied institutions and practices, such as *langar* (communal kitchen),[31] *khande di pahul* (baptismal ceremony),[32] and *karah parshad* (blessed food),[33] explicitly undermine hierarchical distinctions. Those who partake in the *khande di pahul* ceremony are cleansed of their previous identities and reborn as members of the community of the pure. They adopt Sikh surnames devoid of caste affiliation, Kaur (Lioness/Princess) for women and Singh (Lion) for men; and maintain the Five Ks[34]. These Sikhs are now referred to as *amritdhari*—those who keep unshorn hair and have undergone the baptismal ceremony—whereas *kesdhari* are those who keep unshorn hair but have not been baptized, and *sahijdhari* are those who do not keep unshorn hair and have not undergone the baptismal ceremony (Mann 2004, 99). Participation in *langar*, initiation through the *khande di pahul* ceremony, and distribution and eating of *karah prashad* undermine notions of caste- and gender-based ritual purity by ensuring that Sikhs irrespective of caste and gender differences participate communally in embodied religious practices.

Even though Sikhism is committed to eradicating caste- and gender-based inequality, ground-level social realities point to the fact that Sikhs have yet to achieve this goal. Despite attempts to democratize, Sikhism is experienced as uneven and unequal. Despite these egalitarian principles, inclusion in the Sikh community is incomplete and partial. It is also important to note that caste and gender are not experienced uniformly; rather, they intersect to create a varied experience of gendered violence in the Sikh community.[35]

In Sikhism, there is no scriptural sanction for caste distinction, but nonetheless there exists a Sikh caste hierarchy composed of Jats, Khatris, artisan castes, and scheduled castes.[36] Some consider Khatris to be at the top, while others place Jats at the top; these two groups are followed by artisan castes, such as Ramgarhias (carpenters), with scheduled castes, such as Ramdasis and Mazhbis, at the bottom.[37] A large portion of the scheduled caste community is traditionally known as Chamars (leatherworkers), who refer to themselves as Ramdasis or Ravidasis, and Chuhras (sweepers), who refer to themselves as Mazhbis or Rangretas.[38] Unlike their Muslim and Christian counterparts, low-caste Sikhs have the distinction of being included in the list of the scheduled castes.[39]

Sikhism purports to value gender equality; however, even in a community committed to gender equality there is evidence of sexism and gendered violence. While an explicit ban against female infanticide marks a commitment to gender equality, the highly skewed sex ratio (893:1000)[40] among Sikhs indicates continued use of the practice.[41] Other measures of violence against women in Punjab reinforce these findings, such as high rates of female feticide and infanticide, neglect of female children, sexual assault, domestic violence, and dowry murders (Gupta 1987; Chhachhi 1989; Booth and Verma 1992; Sen 1992, 2003; Mutharayappa et al. 1997; Karlekar 2004; Grewal 2008). Socioeconomic measures among Sikhs also indicate gender-based discrimination: 63 percent of women are literate compared to 75 percent of men; and 20 percent of women participate in the labor market compared to 53 percent of men (Indian Census 2011b).[42] Similarly, social norms in Punjab, such as lack of female *granthis* (priests), restrictions on women's religious *seva* (service), and women's restricted relationship with her natal family, also indicate continued sexism (McLeod 1989; Singh 2000; Jakobsh 2006; Shanker 2002; Karlekar 2004; Grewal 2008).

CONCLUSION

An examination of the 2012 gang rape and the subsequent national debates highlights the unpredictability of the political process, explains why political openings for gender equality do not necessarily translate into progressive political change, and illustrates how women experience the Indian state as contradictory. The horrific gang rape and murder and the ensuing national uproar and momentary hope illuminate the contradictory nature of Indian democracy, which constitutionally promises gender equality, yet tragically fails to realize this promise. This analysis challenges the myth that legal institutions are rational, impartial, and neutral in their negotiation of social power, and forces a rethinking of democratic inclusion as a linear, progressive path to full, substantive citizenship.

In the following chapters, I apply a situated approach to citizenship to determine if other spheres of life—civil society, religious community, and home—might be potential sources for more egalitarian social relations. Chapters 4 and 5 uses semi-structured, in-depth interviews with members of the Sikh community to map how one minority religious community in India both upholds exclusionary inclusion and resists it in surprising ways.

Understanding
Exclusionary Inclusion

Sikh Women, Home, and Marriage

When asked about women's place in Sikhism, Rupinder Kaur, a sixty-two-year-old upper-caste woman, directly cites Sikh scriptures to demonstrate that Sikhism renounces notions of female inferiority and impurity: "If you consider this question, then you have to say, 'Then why call her polluted from whom, All great ones [rajas] are born?' This is written in *gurbani* (word of God)." However, within minutes, Rupinder Kaur compares women to insects:[1]

If you consider the question of women's purity, then you have to acknowledge that women are polluted. . . . We consider men to be pure. Women, on the other hand, are insects among insects. Ask me why? See, first of all a woman hasn't even come to her senses and she starts her—you know—menses. This happens when she is a girl. And in the Sikh religion this is considered impure. In the Sikh religion they say that a woman shouldn't engage in prayers when she is impure and she shouldn't come before [Guru Granth] and bow. . . . Second, a woman, to be completely frank, if she is left free, left to her own devices, do you think she can remain pure [a reference to sexual purity]? Men don't even leave an insane woman untouched.

This is neither a woman's fault nor a man's fault. This is how God created women.

For Kaur, the source of women's impurity is twofold—reproduction and sexuality. Women's reproduction, in particular menstruation, is polluting and therefore limits women's access to Sikh scripture. Women's sexuality is also a source of pollution because women's sexuality makes them vulnerable to male sexual assault. Kaur essentializes men and women such that women are by definition inferior to men, and always at risk of sexual assault and violence—a fact that cannot be changed because this is how God created the two sexes.

Rupinder Kaur's comments are representative of a larger contradiction shared by many Sikhs who vehemently oppose sexism as antithetical to Sikhism while simultaneously endorsing gender-based discrimination, exclusion, and violence. What makes this contradiction even more interesting is the fact that a majority of Sikhs, men and women, uphold it. Kaur's comments raise important questions: How do research participants maintain a belief in gender equality while also participating in and advocating for gender-based discrimination, exclusion, and violence? How do research participants make sense of the gap between Sikh ideals of gender equality and Sikh women's lived experience of inequality? Also, how do Sikh men and women define the category of woman? And what are the implications of these definitions? How is sexism defined by participants, and what forms of discrimination are included and excluded in the dominant definition of sexism? These questions matter because they move us beyond a focus on the state and law and explain how exclusionary inclusion operates in civil society and the home. These questions also demonstrate how often taken-for-granted categories, such as "woman" and "sexism," are defined in such a way that they uphold exclusionary inclusion.

In this chapter, I apply a situated approach to citizenship to understand the lived experience of Sikh women in civil society and in the home. To demonstrate that gender equality is defined in a narrow way, I deconstruct research participants' operative meanings of "woman," "equality," and "sexism." I use the feminist strategy of *displacement*—the destabilizing

of existing binaries and oppositions—to show how these categories legitimize women's exclusion and privilege other interests over gender equality
(Waylen et al. 2013, 14). In particular, I follow Linda Alcoff's (2006,
134) claim that "the dilemma facing feminist theorists is that our very self-
definition is grounded in a concept that must be deconstructed and de-
essentialized in all of its aspects."

Through an analysis of interview data, I demonstrate how participants
naturalize gendered citizenship, which results in a demarcation of certain
domains, in particular home and marriage, as the natural space of Sikh
women outside the reach of legal and legislative reform. I argue that institutional indicators and legal status cannot fully account for unequal and
incomplete forms of belonging because they often render the mechanisms
of exclusionary inclusion invisible. In contrast, my analysis of situated
citizenship among Sikh women makes us attuned to women's experience of exclusionary inclusion by showing how the category of woman
is constructed in relation to home and marriage, and how exclusionary
inclusion is naturalized through the following unwritten and informal
rules: (1) women's rights and duties, (2) public policies, (3) women's religiosity, (4) women's purity, and (5) women as perpetual outsiders. Women
experience uneven and partial inclusion in civil society and the private
space of the home. Sikh women do not experience civil society as an
uncoerced space of voluntary associational life, and they do not experience the home as a place of safety, security, and respect. Rather they experience exclusionary inclusion in both these spaces.

Significant change in gendered practices is not highly likely because
research participants (often unintentionally) perpetuate gender-based
discrimination and bias even when most members of the group are genuinely in favor of and committed to gender equality.[2] A majority of Sikhs
understand gender equality and religious autonomy as competing goals,
which makes it difficult to achieve egalitarian gender relations within civil
society and the home. Sikh women are an essential part of formal institutional democracy, but are unable to acquire full, substantive citizenship
because women are understood as restricted to home and marriage.[3]

This analysis suggests that the complex processes of democratic participation and inclusion cannot be solely measured through institutional indicators, formal laws, or religious codes of conduct. These indicators overlook how the practices and processes of exclusionary inclusion operate in civil society and in the home to cause partial belonging and membership. In contrast, my analysis of situated citizenship makes women's experience of exclusionary inclusion visible and demonstrates that neither formal laws nor religious prescriptions guarantee democratic life.

These findings also suggest, contrary to the democratization literature, that Indian democracy is not yet a model democracy because women experience democracy differentially; women do not have the power to be active citizens. Women's inability to acquire full, effective citizenship and democratic inclusion impacts *all* citizens. Women's participation in civil society is key for improving democratic policy responsiveness, especially to progressive social policies.[4] Also, women's participation is crucial because "only a democratic civil society can sustain a democratic state" (Walzer 1991, 302).[5]

When asked about gender, a majority of participants adhere to a Sikh narrative of egalitarianism while engaging in discriminatory practices against Sikh women. Most participants are able to discuss their personal discriminatory beliefs and practices while maintaining a commitment to gender equality by defining sexism in a narrow way, which emphasizes certain forms of discrimination and obscures others. According to a Sikh narrative of egalitarianism, gender-based discrimination is no longer a problem in the Sikh community because Sikhism at its founding and through its institutions eliminated sexism.

Thus, the following questions arise: how do participants account for the vast discrepancies between Sikh men and women, if, for them, gender-based discrimination does not exist? How do Sikh men and women experience and interpret sexism in a community that denies its very existence? More specifically, how do participants live within the contradiction between a hierarchically organized gender-based society and a religious commitment to gender equality? I argue that a majority of participants explain the structural position of Sikh women through a series of gendered norms that minimize their own participation in discriminatory practices.

The goal of this analysis is to explore the contradictions between participants' claims to gender equality and their sexist opinions, behaviors, and beliefs. By analyzing the relationship between expressed commitment to gender equality and sexist practices, I focus attention on the embodied, lived experience of citizenship in a liberal democracy. By situating citizenship, I demonstrate the context from which participants develop an understanding of and enact exclusionary inclusion, which results in citizenship's failed promise of equality. There is a complex relationship between religious and formal laws, and participants' practices, opinions, and behaviors, which calls into question any simple correlation between formal, legal status and lived experience.

In the following sections, I discuss interview and participant observation findings, with attention to the ways participants define sexism, minimize their own participation in discrimination, and construct the category of woman in relation to home and marriage, and to the five primary ways participants naturalize a gendered construction of citizenship—women's rights and duties, public policies, women's religiosity, women's purity, and women as perpetual outsiders. I conclude by discussing the implications of these findings for the study of democracy, citizenship, and gender.

SIKH NARRATIVE OF EGALITARIANISM

Nearly all participants believe in and commit themselves to a Sikh narrative of egalitarianism because for them it is divinely ordained. Yet the task of living in accordance with a narrative of egalitarianism is not a simple matter; it is mediated by debates internal to Sikh religious tradition, and by the particular material conditions of participants' lives. Part of my goal in this chapter is to explore the limits and failings of formal citizenship, as well as the day-to-day context through which these limitations and failings are constructed, reinforced, and challenged. The aim, in other words, is to map the mechanisms of exclusionary inclusion that result in conditional belonging and membership.

A Sikh narrative of egalitarianism, which is upheld by scholars and devotees alike, most often references three topics: (1) the Guru Period, (2) Sikh scripture, and (3) Sikh institutions. Scholars and followers reference these three topics as evidence of gender equality and Sikh exceptionalism. Sikh exceptionalism asserts that the problem of gender discrimination, exclusion, and violence exists elsewhere—in other communities, not among Sikhs—and what is required is a return to Sikh scripture and institutions, a return to a true Sikhism.

Many scholars and research participants point to the Guru Period—extending from the birth of Guru Nanak in 1469 to the death of the tenth guru in 1708—as the golden age of Sikh women's equality, which was corrupted by pernicious Hindu, Muslim, and later British patriarchal culture (Kaur 1990; I. J. Singh 1998; N. Singh 1993, 2008, 2009). Doris Jakobsh (2006, 187) finds fault with this particular approach and argues that references to a Sikh golden age of women's equality obscures present-day issues of gender inequality: "The 'golden age' of Sikh women during the Guru period is iterated and reiterated and scriptural passages highlighting women's equal access to liberation along with injunctions against women's impurity are consistently upheld. When the issue of inequality is raised, the raison d'être for such inequalities is quickly deflected to the religious milieu surrounding Sikhism."

Many scholars and research participants directly cite passages from the Guru Granth to substantiate a narrative of egalitarianism.[6] The passage cited most frequently by scholars and participants comes from Guru Nanak's hymn, in which Nanak asks, "Then why call her inferior/polluted from whom / All great ones [rajas] are born?" (Guru Granth, 473). This is a line from Guru Nanak's larger hymn:

Of woman are we born, of woman conceived,
To woman engaged, to woman married.
Woman we befriend, by woman do civilizations continue.
When a woman dies, a woman is sought for.

It is through woman that order is maintained.

Then why call her inferior/polluted[7] from whom

All great ones are born?

Woman is born of woman;

None is born but of woman.

The One, who is Eternal, alone is unborn.

Says Nanak, that tongue alone is blessed

That utters the praise of the One.

Such alone will be acceptable at the Court of the True One.

(Guru Granth, 473)[8]

Some scholars, like Nikky Guninder Kaur Singh (1993, 2008, 2009), point to this particular hymn as evidence of gender equality. Guru Nanak's questioning of the stigma and taboo associated with women's reproductive power is interpreted by Singh as an acknowledgment of menstrual bleeding as an essential, natural process, one free of pollution and stigma. According to Gurnam Singh (2006, 148), Nanak's representation of the disciple as bride and God as groom allows Nanak to (1) disrupt the powerful male-female binarism and (2) affirm female sexuality, thus demonstrating a commitment to radical equality. Other scholars, such as Gurinder Singh Mann (2001, 102–103), argue that "women, as part of the divine creation, could not be the carriers of pollution . . . for Vahiguru [God] views men and women as equals."

Doris Jakobsh (2000, 2003, 2006) rejects claims of women's radical equality in Sikh scripture. According to Jakobsh (2000, 270), "Although Sikh apologetics repeatedly insist that men and women are inherently equal in the Sikh worldview, in reality, historical writings say virtually nothing about women." Jakobsh also argues that Nanak's hymns can be read as contradictory because, at times, women are respected as procreators and, at other times, they are described as manifestations of maya and the source of corruption and degradation. Similarly, Rajkumari Shanker (2002, 118–120) finds that the Granth emphasizes female subservience, obedience, docility, and dedication, while these same attributes are discouraged in men, thus undermining notions of gender equality.

Lastly, scholars and participants cite Sikh institutions as evidence of a narrative of egalitarianism. In particular, they point to *langar* (communal kitchen), *khande di pahul* (baptismal ceremony), *karah parshad* (blessed food), and *pangat* (sitting in a status-free line) as institutions and practices that undermine hierarchical distinctions based on age, gender, caste, and social status (see chapter 3). They also point to ethical codes of conduct, from the eighteenth century and onward, including the twentieth-century Sikh Rahit Maryada, which explicitly forbid and denounce purdah (female veiling), female infanticide, sati, and dowry, and encourage widow remarriage (Mann 2001). Nikky Guninder Kaur Singh (2008, 333) finds that Sikhism, as envisioned by Nanak and institutionalized through the Rahit Maryada, "grants full equality to men and women in all spheres—religious, political, domestic, and economic." According to Singh (2000, 67), Nanak, the founder of Sikhism, elevated women to a position of equality by rejecting "all austere and ascetic practices, elaborate forms of worship, and rites and ceremonies that segregated society on the basis of religion, caste, race, class, or gender." Singh (1993, 254) argues that in Nanak's new community, men and women enjoyed complete equality.

Others, like Doris Jakobsh, challenge this view. Jakobsh (2000, 270) argues that the idea of gender equality is best understood as a myth because Sikh history is largely silent when it comes to gender. According to Navdeep Mandair (2005, 49–50), Sikh rejection of misogynistic practices during the Singh Sabha movement (established in 1873) should be understood as a strategy to differentiate between Sikhism and Hinduism, not a means to create gender equality: "It is not obvious that this repudiation of misogynistic practices facilitates a sanction of gender equality given that the real purpose of this expression of censure is to highlight the fundamental degeneracy of a [Hindu] culture that advocates such customs."

According to W. H. McLeod (1989, 108), theoretically women are regarded as equals, but "their actual status falls short of the theoretical claim." McLeod also argues that women's right to participate in religious rituals is generally recognized, especially when compared to women who belong to other religions in India. In reality, however, men enjoy effective authority over the Sikh faith and in the Sikh community (McLeod

1989, 108–109; Jakobsh 2006, 188). Similarly, Jakobsh (2006, 188) finds that "women have the right to become granthis (custodians of gurdwaras who also act as caretakers of the Guru Granth Sahib, the sacred scripture of the Sikhs), ragis (professional musicians of kirtan), and panj piares (the five beloved who administer the initiation rite), but there is no mention of the fact that women rarely, if ever, become granthis or panj piares."

Minimizing and Distancing Sexism

Research participants use a Sikh narrative of egalitarianism, including references to the Guru Period, Sikh scripture, and Sikh institutions, to assert Sikh exceptionalism by claiming that the problem of gender-based discrimination, exclusion, and violence exists in other places, in other communities—not among Sikhs. I find that research participants' dominant conception of equality emphasizes that (1) women were unequal prior to the founding of Sikhism; and (2) women's equality was secured and enshrined by Guru Nanak with the founding of the Sikh Panth, with the establishment of Sikh institutions and practices, and through Sikh scripture and ethical codes. Such claims allow participants to distance themselves from discriminatory, exclusionary, and violent attitudes and actions by shifting responsibility onto others, to minimize women's current-day experiences of sexism by shifting focus to the golden age of Sikh equality, and to minimize their own participation in maintaining gendered power structures by naturalizing exclusionary inclusion.

When asked about women's treatment in Sikhism, a majority of participants state that Sikh women are equal to Sikh men and Sikh women enjoy respect in the Sikh faith.[9] Nearly all participants—irrespective of gender, caste, age, and educational differences—adhere to this narrative. Hardev Singh Saini, a forty-three-year-old, educated, scheduled-caste man who works as a police constable, and Balbir Kaur, a sixty-year-old, minimally educated, upper-caste woman who is a housewife, both state that Sikhism eliminated sexism:

Hardev Singh Saini: The Sikh religion gives women the utmost respect—a good amount of respect.

Balbir Kaur: The Sikh religion gives women a very high degree of respect. Guru Nanak Devji said woman gives birth to rajas, and therefore she deserves full respect and reverence.

Research participants simultaneously avowed their commitment to a Sikh narrative of egalitarianism and discriminated against women. For example, on occasion, when I conducted interviews with married women, their husbands would take over the interview and speak for their wives. Often husbands would answer questions *for* their wives, and the wives would take on a more submissive and docile position (both attitudinal and physical) when their husbands spoke. Husbands often expressed their commitment to gender equality as part and parcel of their Sikh faith, while silencing their wives during the interview process. What I saw and observed was in tension with participants' expressed beliefs.

When asked how women are treated in Sikhism, a majority of participants also claimed that prior to the Guru Period women were relegated to a position of inferiority. Guru Nanak, however, provided women with social and religious uplift, thereby eliminating any problems associated with women's impurity, inferiority, and inequality. For example, Bachittar Singh Walia, a forty-year-old upper-caste man, states:

In the Sikh religion women are given full respect and reverence. During the time of Sri Guru Nanak Devji there was a great deal of disrespect and mistreatment of women. At that point, Sri Guru Nanak Devji, for the protection of women, went so far as to say, "Then why call her inferior/polluted from whom, / All great ones [rajas] are born" (Guru Granth, 473). It is the woman's womb that gives birth to rajas and maharajas, so how can we say anything negative about a woman? At that point in time women were thought of as inferior—they were considered to be at a very low level—and Sri Guru Nanakji made some fantastic changes and gave women their due respect and reverence.

For Walia and others, the problem of women's inequality existed prior to Sikhism. This is a problem that has been solved, for Sikhs, and now Sikh women enjoy respect, equality, and reverence.

In addition to citing scripture, participants also refer to Sikh institutions as evidence of women's equality. Participants, like Surinder Singh, a twenty-two-year-old upper-caste man, discuss purdah and sati to substantiate a Sikh narrative of egalitarianism:

The practice of purdah was eliminated by the Sikh religion. The Sikh religion was the first to take this step. Next it was the British Raj that said that this practice should stop. The Sikh religion did a lot to eliminate both the practice of sati and purdah. Sikhs said that both these practices should come to a stop.

Singh and others argue that Sikhs were the first to question, challenge, and ultimately eliminate sexist and misogynistic practices. After the Sikhs, it was the British who called for the abolition of these practices.[10]

Other participants substantiate a Sikh narrative of egalitarianism by discussing women's access to and engagement with the Guru Granth. Hardev Singh Saini points to women's participation in Sukhmani Seva Societies (devotional organizations) as a manifestation of women's equal role in Sikh religious life:

Now women are active. Like in our colony, a Sukhmani Seva Society has been created by women; so a majority of the time when there are Sukhmani Sahib prayers in someone's home, women usually conduct these prayers. The *granthi* doesn't do it; the women do.

For Saini, the creation of women's Sukhmani Seva Societies demonstrates women's equality and participation in public religious life.[11]

Research participants define sexism, discrimination, inferiority, and inequality as problems of the past that were eliminated during the Guru Period, thus freeing Sikhs of any present-day responsibility for continued sexism. By constructing equality as something that has already been achieved, research participants overlook current-day indicators of SGBV—such as such as high rates of female feticide and infanticide, neglect of female children, rape and sexual assault, domestic violence, and dowry murders—and opt to focus on gendered violence and gendered norms, which were predominant during the Guru Period, yet have limited salience for women's everyday lives.

Also, research participants define women's participation in Sikh institutions, rites, and rituals as equal. However, the very nature of this participation is restricted and qualified.[12] For example, in Hardev Singh Saini's example of devotional organizations, the female members of the local Sukhmani Seva Society have access to the Guru Granth, thus enabling them to engage in public recitation of the scripture.[13] Yet these women are denied access to the title of professional keeper and reader of the Granth. According to Saini, "The *granthi* doesn't [recite prayers]; the women do." This characterization creates two separate and mutually exclusive categories of woman and *granthi*, thus foreclosing the possibility of female *granthis*. Women have the capacity to conduct prayers, but they are denied the official title and position, thus limiting their access to and authority in religious, economic, and public life.

Scholars of Sikh and Punjab studies point to Sikh history, scripture, and institutions as evidence that Sikh women are equal members of the Sikh community; however, they do not ask how Sikhs interpret, enforce, and experience this abstract commitment to equality. Similarly, research participants use a Sikh narrative of egalitarianism to assert Sikh exceptionalism by claiming that the problem of gender discrimination, exclusion, and violence exists elsewhere, in other communities, not among Sikhs. Such claims allow participants to distance themselves from sexist attitudes and actions by shifting responsibility onto others, and to minimize women's current-day experiences of sexism by shifting focus to the golden age of Sikh equality. What remains unexamined by both scholars and participants is the extent to which religious laws and institutions effectively achieve gender equality and engender behavioral and attitudinal changes.

UNDERSTANDING EXCLUSIONARY INCLUSION: SIKH WOMEN, HOME, AND MARRIAGE

Through an analysis of semi-structured, in-depth interview data, I make visible Sikh women's experience of exclusionary inclusion, and examine women's unequal and uneven experience in civil society and the home. By situating citizenship, I deconstruct participants' operative meanings of "woman" to illustrate that participants construct and understand the category in relation to home and marriage. I also find that participants naturalize women's partial inclusion through the following norms: women's rights and duties, public policies, women's religiosity, women's purity, and women as perpetual outsiders. These gendered norms (except for purity and pollution) are dominant among a majority of Sikhs, irrespective of gender, caste, age, and educational differences, and I rely on one example of each theme to illustrate a general trend in the responses. Lastly, I analyze the interview data with attention to how participants understand and negotiate key elements of citizenship: rights and duties, belonging, and participation.

Women's Rights and Duties

Most participants understand women as partial members of their communities with limited rights and duties. Participants' expectations about appropriate gender roles limit women's participation to the private space of the home, as nonworkers, defined in relation to men and marriage.[14] When I asked women about their participation in civic and associational life, their responses, unlike men's responses, were centered on the home. Female participants understood their engagement in civil society in terms of distance from their home, which limited their participation and belonging to their own neighborhood. For example, female participants often stated that the local *gurdwara* (Sikh temple) was too far from their home and that they feared walking to the *gurdwara*. Many female participants preferred to engage in associational life within half a mile to a mile radius from their home because they feared walking beyond this distance. Also, many women feared crossing major roads within this radius. Men's discussion of associational life did not include geographical restriction, concern about transportation, or fear about safety. Fear about safety significantly undermines women's ability to move freely, to use public spaces, and to participate in associational life, the labor market, and educational life.[15]

Democratization scholars point to the Fundamental Rights as evidence that Indian women are full citizens, but they do not ask how individuals experience these rights. In the abstract, Sikh women enjoy freedom of speech, association, and travel; however, interview responses illustrate that lack of safety, both experienced and perceived, determine whether Sikh women can exercise their rights. A situated analysis of citizenship illuminates dimensions of Sikh women's lives that traditional democratic scholars overlook and points to the failed promise of equality.

Participants like Surinder Singh define women's rights and duties in relation to home and marriage:

> Ladies' . . . devotion is to give children life. This is their greatest devotion—that they raise their children. Their biggest *seva* [service] is to their children; mothers are everything for their children.

By emphasizing women's *seva* as mothers, Singh obscures questions of Sikh women's participation and belonging outside the home. Questions about women's equality outside of the home are never asked because women's greatest *seva* is equated with the home, marriage, and motherhood. This definition of woman has the practical consequence of limiting and restricting women's access to civil society required to support democracy. Often these restrictions are upheld within the privacy of the home through intimate kinship. Similarly, Jyoti Grewal (2008, 169) finds that in Punjab, "the idea of women being involved in matters outside the home continues to be . . . discouraged. A woman's work is within the chaardivari, literally 'the four walls' of her home." This definition of women as mothers at the center of the household also ignores working-class, often lower-caste, women who work outside the home and neglects women without children.[16]

By deconstructing Singh's operative meaning of "woman," we find that he defines the category in relation to home and marriage, which justifies discrimination against women, and demarcates the home as the natural space of Sikh women beyond the reach of legal and legislative reform. Interview responses like Singh's reveal the mechanisms that construct and maintain exclusionary inclusion, mechanisms that conventional institutional indicators of democracy render invisible.

Public Policies

Some participants understand women's rights as limited, especially in inheritance and property. The 2005 amendment to the Hindu Succession Act (which also governs Sikhs) enabled daughters to inherit joint family property. Udham Singh, a thirty-three-year-old scheduled-caste man, describes the 2005 amendment in the following way:

> The state is now saying that girls have a legal right to a share of their parents' land. . . . The law itself is wrong. The main hand in female feticide is the state's because the state made this law. . . . Let's say there is a falling-out between the sister and her brothers. Well, then she sells her parental property and destroys her brothers. And she becomes the owner of her parents' land and of her in-laws' land; she is the owner of the old property and the new property. . . . The state causes the killing that is occurring of young girls . . . the state is responsible for these killings. If this law were to change, then this [killing] would stop.

Participants like Singh blame the very public policies designed to protect women for continued female feticide and murder of young girls. Singh argues that the state is responsible for women's murders because the state amended the Hindu Succession Act to harm men and benefit women because these policies can potentially transform women's economic and social position vis-a-vis inheritance. Men like Singh justify violence against women as a means to protect their own economic security.

Often we assume that constitutions and statutes determine inheritance and property rights, but an analysis of the interview data reveals that private citizens gender property rights through interpretation and enforcement at the local level within families and communities. Localized practices in the home—violence against women, female feticide, and dowry murders—determine whether Sikh women can effectively exercise their formal rights.[17] Democratization scholars often point to the existence of certain laws and statutes to argue that Indian women are full citizens, while Sikh and Punjab studies scholars frequently point to Sikh ethical codes as evidence of women's equality; however, these scholars do not ask how these laws and codes are enforced on women's bodies. What remains unexamined is the tension between legal and religious reforms and gendered norms and unwritten rules.

In Singh's interview response, the category of woman is multiple, yet constrained. Singh acknowledges women's multiple roles as daughter, wife, and daughter-in-law. However, in doing so, he defines women in relation to men and marriage. What is implicit in Singh's response is the definition of women as either "good" or "bad." For example, a good sister would not fall out with her brothers; she would forgo her property rights to maintain strong familial ties with her natal family, whereas, a bad sister would not only break off ties with her own brothers, but would also make a grab at her brother's land and her in-laws' land, and by doing so she would economically and socially destroy both her natal and married families. Singh's response also privileges middle-class women over working-class women because "dowry-murders and inheritance disputes are predominantly a middle-class phenomenon" (Narayan 1997, 92). In Singh's response, the simultaneous operation of sexism, casteism, and classism obscures the experience of working-class, lower-caste women, justifies violence against all women, and genders property rights.

Singh's interview response also speaks to gendered patterns of land-ownership in India. In legal terms, women enjoy extensive rights to inherit land, but in practice, most are disinherited (Kapur and Cossman 1999). According to participants like Surjit Kaur, a twenty-eight-year-old upper-caste woman, women's rights "are written in the books but aren't practiced":

> People don't actually give their daughters land; however, legally daughters do have a right to their parents' land . . . once again, the rights are all words. . . . Practically speaking, girls don't receive any land from their parents, and they don't receive any land from their in-laws.

Women's command over immovable assets is important for women's economic and social well-being because it alleviates poverty, increases economic and social security, increases the likelihood of children surviving, attending school and receiving healthcare, reduces destitution following widowhood, and reduces spousal desertion.[18] Namita Datta (2006, 293) finds that property rights "increase women's participation in decision making, access to knowledge and information about public matters, sense of security, self-esteem, and the respect that they receive from their spouses." Women's property rights guarantee social citizenship, which, in turn, enables women to actualize their political and civil rights.

Some participants, like Udham Singh, characterize the protection of women's property rights as a threat to men. However, according to Surjit Kaur, women are victims who are routinely disinherited by their own families in the private space of the home. Democratization scholars point to laws as evidence for women's full citizenship without recognizing the gap between law on the books and lived reality. An analysis of situated citizenship challenges these conclusions by pointing out processes of exclusionary inclusion that traditional democratic indicators, such as laws, statutes, and constitutions, overlook.

Women's Religiosity

Many participants, like Beena Kaur, a sixty-five-year-old upper-caste woman, conceive of women's rights and duties, belonging, and participation as contingent upon their religiosity.

> Nowadays, forget a woman wearing her *dupata* [scarf] on her head. . . . The *dupata* has flown away. Sleeveless arms, very, very small blouses . . . The meaning of this is that today's woman has become shameless. She is showing off her body, like many Hindustani women. And men are becoming hunters. The men are hungry. Guru Gobind Singh Maharaj said, "Read *bani* [the word of God] and wear *bana* [religious dress]" . . . a modest *salwar-kameez* [long-shirt and pants], and a *dupata* on one's head. . . . If a girl is herself strong, if a girl dresses well . . . then no man has the nerve to even get close to this girl. A woman is respected in our religion. . . . However, if we ourselves have turned on our proper attire, then how is that the guru's fault?

Kaur's focus on women's religiosity allows her to shift all culpability for SGBV to women themselves by stating that women's adherence to proper attire, which functions as a visible marker of women's modesty, determines their access to the three key elements of citizenship. A modest woman, according to Kaur, wears *salwar kameez* and a *dupata* on her head, and any deviation from this *bana* is equated with a shameful woman who deserves mistreatment.[19] In Kaur's response, the category of religion and gender intersect to create divisions between Sikh women, characterized as modest (if they adhere to religious prescriptions), and Indian/Hindustani women, characterized as shameless.

Sikh participants and Indian politicians both use the norm of women's religiosity (see chapter 3). Some Sikh research participants justify and mandate SGBV by claiming that Sikh women who forgo modest Sikh attire and adopt shameless Hindustani attire deserve sexual assault, while Indian politicians claim that Indian women who reject Hindustani modest dress and adopt Westernized clothing also deserve to be assaulted. A similar pattern appears in both responses. Both Sikh research participants and Indian politicians claim that the problem of gendered violence exists in other places, in other communities, in other cultures, and therefore a return to Hindustani culture and Hindu religion free of Western influence is necessary, or a return to Sikhism free of a Hindu influence is vital. Sikh women, in particular, find themselves in a double bind as they are forced to navigate between multiple sets of norms—Sikh regulation of dress, Hindustani norms of dress, and Westernized clothing—which are policed within the home and in civil society. Kaur's response points to the fact that the category of woman is not homogenous; rather women are differentiated by and negotiate between minority and majority religious norms, global norms and trends, familial expectations, and individual desire and autonomy.

Kaur's response also demonstrates that women are victims and agents of gendered violence. Kaur assumes that "women are the objects of sexual desire and men the desiring subjects, an assumption that justifies the injunction that women should 'hide their charms' when in public so as not to excite the libidinal energies of men" (Mahmood 2005, 110). Kaur frees men of any responsibility for "hunting" women, while legitimizing SGBV. Kaur's response disadvantages women by assigning them the burden of maintaining the community's purity through their dress, which in turn limits women's access to public spaces. A focus on women's religiosity enables Kaur and others to justify, and perhaps mandate, gendered violence by normalizing men's role as sexual predator and women's role as sexual object in the public sphere.

Democratization scholars point to formal rights as evidence for Indian women's equality. This analysis examines how participants' expectations about religious norms are in tension with these formal rights. An analysis of situated citizenship makes visible gendered religious norms that determine who can exercise their rights and who is most vulnerable to violence. Such an analysis explains how and why women experience civil society as dangerous, threatening, and violent. This analysis also demonstrates that for some research participants, community purity, solidarity, and autonomy trumps women's safety and equality.

Women's Purity and Pollution

Many female participants understand women as partial members of the Sikh community with limited rights and duties because of the logic of purity and pollution. It is important to note that only female participants discussed the theme of purity and pollution. And most women spoke of these issues in a hushed voice, thus underscoring the shame, secrecy, and embarrassment of female impurity associated with menstruation and childbirth. For example, Balbir Kaur explains women's limited rights and duties by emphasizing female impurity:

> First of all, the reason that there are restrictions against women being *granthis* is because women aren't capable of such a high degree of purity. Women can't have the same degree of purity as men and that's why women aren't allowed to get ahead and take the lead. . . . For example, women lose their purity monthly [menstruation]. . . . It comes to my mind that this is perhaps the reason that women aren't allowed to be *granthis*.

Balbir Kaur and others explain the lack of female *granthis* by stating that menstruation and childbirth cause pollution, and women should not sit before the Guru Granth when polluted, and therefore, women must accept that they cannot be *granthis* because they are incapable of attaining the same degree of purity as men. In short, participants shift responsibility for the perpetuation of misogynistic practices away from individual, institutional, or structural forces to female reproduction and biology, and therefore to an essentialized and immutable gendered difference.

Guru Nanak, the founder of Sikhism, unequivocally rejected notions of female pollution associated with menstruation and childbirth. This initial vision was institutionalized and codified in Sikh *rahit* from the eighteenth century onward, which explicitly stresses women's full participation in religious life. Nonetheless, many female participants believe that menstruation and childbirth are polluting and, therefore, that women lack the purity necessary to enter *gurdwaras* and sit before and read from the Guru Granth. This logic in turn forecloses the possibility of female *granthis* because women cannot attain the purity needed to be a professional reader and caretaker of Sikh scripture.

When I asked how women come to know about issues of purity and pollution, Santokh Kaur, a forty-six-year-old upper-caste woman, stated, "Women are told about this, my child, by the female elders in the home. There is an emphasis on being clean and pure people, especially when you go the *gurdwara sahib* [Sikh temple]." Knowledge of purity and pollution does not come from scriptural text, religious *rahit*, or religious *katha* (commentary on sacred verses); rather, it is transmitted within the home from older women to younger ones. Older women teach younger women about purity and pollution, police the bodies and behaviors of younger women, and ensure "appropriate" behavior as it relates to purity and pollution. A situated approach to citizenship reveals how exclusionary inclusion is maintained and perpetuated in the private space of the home through intimate kinship relations.

In these interview responses, the category of woman is defined through sexuality and reproduction, which is monitored, controlled, and policed by other women, in particular older women within kinship ties. In doing so, participants shift responsibility for the perpetuation of sexist practices and gendered norms to female reproduction and biology, which is characterized as immutable. Female participants police women's bodies through the logic of purity and pollution, and, ultimately, uphold exclusionary inclusion.

Often scholars point to formal rights and scriptural passages as evidence for women's equality. This analysis examines how participants' views about purity and pollution are in tension with these formal rights and religious prescriptions. An analysis of Sikh situated citizenship makes visible gendered norms that determine who can exercise their rights, who can access religious space, and who is considered pure.

Women as Perpetual Outsiders

Many participants describe women as perpetual outsiders who do not belong in either their natal or married home. Women's position as perpetual outsider stems from the fact that parents regard their sons as their social security, financial insurance, and religious functionaries, who are essential for carrying on the family name and property, whereas they characterize daughters as beautiful commodities and investments that will eventually be lost to someone else.[20] Malavika Karlekar (2004, 318) argues, "Nothing describes the transient nature of a girl's brief life span in her parent's home or her inherent worth better than the north-Indian saying that girl is *paraya dhan* or another's wealth. It not only establishes the very notion of belonging but also that, a girl is wealth (dhan) which belongs ultimately elsewhere (paraya)." Likewise, the Sangtin Writers and Richa Nagar (2006, 44) find that "sometimes it was our *mayaka* [natal home] that embraced us as its own, and sometimes it was our *sasural* [married home]. And sometimes, despite having these two homes, we continued to feel that there was not a corner or place in our lives that we could truly call our own." Similarly, Veena Das (2007, 66) finds that the daughter is a "permanent exile" in Punjabi life, and has few rights or entitlements vis-à-vis her natal or married family.

Many participants, like Santokh Kaur, define women and girls as perpetual outsiders:

> But people still engage in [infanticide] because some people have four or five girls, and then say that with boys our name lives on, our roots keep growing, and girls are destined for someone's home, someone's family.

In Kaur's narrative two factors are salient: (1) the birth order of children,[21] and (2) an understanding of girls as perpetual outsiders. Boys are defined as the source of familial growth, whereas girls are characterized as outsiders who do not belong in their natal homes. Kaur's characterization of girl children as perpetual outsiders, as aliens in their own homes, assumes that girls will leave their natal homes and therefore will never contribute to the social, financial, and religious well-being of their families. Participants define the category of woman as property, commodity, and wealth to be exchanged (unequally) through the institution of marriage from one home to another. By defining women and girls as a depreciating property, participants legitimize SGBV, including female feticide and infanticide, and dowry murders.

Dharamvir Singh, a thirty-five-year-old scheduled-caste man, provides an example of this norm of girls as perpetual outsiders from his own family:

> Even though many girls are more capable than boys, they aren't given a chance; they aren't given support. I can give you an example of this from my own home. My brother has two girls, and he is going to put a stop to their education once they complete plus-two [twelfth grade]. And his son doesn't know anything—he is intellectually dull—but my brother says, "I will educate my son. After the girls finish plus-two, then it's time for their weddings and marriages; they will go to their homes."

According to Dharamvir Singh, his brother does not plan to educate his daughters beyond high school even though they show great potential. Singh's brother justifies his decision by stating that after his daughters complete twelfth grade, it is time for them to marry so they can go to their homes. In this response, the daughters are characterized as outsiders, and, therefore, any decision regarding their future, including education, is determined with this fact in mind. According to this logic, if a father provides his daughter with education, then this education will benefit his daughter's in-laws because her in-laws' home is her true home. However, any and all education provided to a son will directly benefit a father because his son will remain with him and support him through his old age. By characterizing girls and women as perpetual outsiders, participants justify violence and discrimination against girls and women and foreclose the possibility of an alternative conceptualization of the relationship between women and their natal and married families.[22]

Democratization scholars point to the Fundamental Rights as evidence that Indian women are full citizens, while Sikh studies scholars point to scripture and institutions as proof that Sikh women are equal. Both literatures overlook the mechanisms and processes that characterize girls and women as perpetual foreigners, who do not belong in either their natal or married homes, and as property and wealth to be owned, exchanged, exploited, and destroyed through the institution of marriage. By adopting a more expansive definition of the political—which emphasizes studying processes and experiences outside of the state and beyond the law—I examine the tension between claims to gender equality and women's experience as perpetually unequal, and I explain how informal gendered norms and unwritten rules justify and perpetuate women's unequal status and determine their partial citizenship rights.

Challenging Exclusionary Inclusion: Man-Dominated Society

In this section, I examine the interview responses of a very small group of women who are younger, highly educated, and active in the workforce or plan to be active, and who acknowledge and challenge exclusionary inclusion. In chapter 5, I discuss another group of women, members of devotional organizations, who also acknowledge and challenge exclusionary inclusion.

Paramjit Kaur Sidhu's interview responses provide some insight on how individuals make sense of everyday experiences of gender-based discrimination in a community that denies the very existence of gender-based discrimination, exclusion, and violence. Sidhu, a twenty-two-year-old upper-caste woman who is a private school teacher, challenges a narrative of Sikh egalitarianism and the norms that naturalize exclusionary inclusion by discussing how Sikh women are reminded, on a daily basis, of their outsider and inferior position:

When a woman has a daughter, other people will say, "Oh no, why did she have a daughter?" They will continue to harass [the mother] and mistreat her. People say it's her fault; they say, "Why did you have a daughter?" But how is it the woman's fault alone? And let's say the woman does have a daughter; well, then, she won't receive as much respect. Even if [in-laws] accept the daughter—"Fine, you had a daughter, it's fine"—the mother never gets full respect. She will always be harassed about it, ridiculed about it.

According to Sidhu, a woman's place in her in-laws' home, the degree of respect and love she receives, and her personal status are tied to her capacity to birth sons. And if a woman does not satisfy the preference for sons, then she is reminded of her inferiority on a daily basis through rumors, gossip, and ridicule.[23] Sidhu's response challenges a narrative of egalitarianism by demonstrating how a woman's status is tied to her capacity to bear sons. Sidhu's response also demonstrates the fact that Sikh women are perpetual outsiders in their natal and married homes because their rights and duties, belonging, and participation are partial, limited, and restricted. What underlies Sidhu's response is a recognition and challenge of sexist practices, such as son preference.

Surjit Kaur, who is a practicing attorney, makes sense of everyday experiences of gender-based discrimination by acknowledging that Sikh women are treated better than women in other religions; however, she quickly points out that gender-based discrimination and exclusion exist in the Sikh community. For example, Kaur says, "If you go to the main location of Sikhism [the Golden Temple], women are not allowed to participate in *seva*." When asked why this is the case, Kaur discusses male domination and power:

The logic is simple; we live in a man-dominated society. Those who are in positions of power—those who are at the center—are men, and they want to retain their power. There aren't many ladies in these positions. It is true that it hasn't been written anywhere that women can't participate in *seva*. However, it is also the case that none of our gurus were women; they were all men. A woman could have been guru. But from the beginning, man domination is the norm. Ladies' rights are simply in the books; they aren't actually put in practice.

Kaur acknowledges that within Sikhism women enjoy the abstract right to participate in *seva*, but she also states that women's equality has yet to be achieved. For example, Kaur states that "none of our gurus were women; they were all men." Kaur uses this concrete example of male dominance to demonstrate that women's rights exist in the abstract in Sikh scriptural and Indian legal texts, but are not actuated.

Kaur also discusses the fact that Sikh men are in positions of power— they are at the center of institutional power, and they want to retain this power. For Kaur, male domination of key Sikh institutions creates and reinforces male domination in the Sikh community even though this domination is scripturally and legally prohibited. Male domination is the norm in Sikh institutions, yet these very institutions are upheld as evidence of gender equality.

Kaur also shares her personal experience to demonstrate that women's rights are abstract notions, not concrete realities. Kaur, a widow with a five-year-old son, explains that when her husband passed away, her in-laws wrote an erroneous will claiming that Kaur and her husband had bad relations and all of the property should be transferred to the in-laws. According to Kaur, she went through a difficult, multiyear litigation process to gain her right to her husband's property. In the end, Kaur was denied access to her husband's property; rather, it was transferred to her five-year-old son. In this particular case, Kaur, a widow and mother, was disinherited, while her male son was rewarded. Effectively Kaur has no right to property, and her access to property is always mediated through a male family member (her husband and her son). Kaur's experience demonstrates that formally women enjoy extensive rights to inherit land, but in practice, most are disinherited. Sidhu's and Kaur's interview responses provide some insight on how Sikh women experience, understand, and negotiate everyday experiences of gender-based discrimination.

CONCLUSION

An analysis of ethnographic data reveals several consistent reactions to the issue of gender and sexism in the Sikh community. First, nearly all participants state that sexism is not a salient issue in the Sikh community even though these same participants express discriminatory beliefs and participate in discriminatory practices against women. Second, a majority of participants substantiate their belief in gender equality through a Sikh narrative of egalitarianism, which emphasizes the Guru Period, Sikh scripture, and Sikh institutions. And third, a majority of participants explain the structural position of Sikh women through a series of gendered norms that minimize their own participation in discriminatory practices and naturalize exclusionary inclusion: (1) women's rights and duties, (2) public policies, (3) women's religiosity, (4) women's purity, and (5) women as perpetual outsiders.

These findings demonstrate that Sikh women experience exclusionary inclusion in civil society and in the home. They do not experience civil society as solely a space of voluntary association; and they do not experience the home as completely safe and secure. These findings also show that significant change is unlikely because research participants (often unintentionally) perpetuate exclusionary inclusion by elevating community solidarity and religious autonomy over gender equality, even when most are genuinely in favor of and committed to gender equality.

Democratization scholars point to institutional indicators and formal law to argue that Indian democracy is consolidated and Indian women are full citizens, while Sikh and Punjab studies scholars point to the Guru Period, Sikh scriptures, and Sikh institutions to argue that Sikh women are full and equal members of the Sikh community. I argue that formal and religious indicators fail to tell the full story because they overlook mediating forces, which result in uneven, unequal, and impartial membership and belonging in a liberal democracy. In contrast, my analysis of situated citizenship shows how the category of woman is constructed in relation to home and marriage, and maps how exclusionary inclusion is

naturalized. What I find is a continuum of gendered violence with violent sexual assault and rape at one end, and gendered norms and informal
rules determining who has access to food, healthcare, education, inheritance, and property rights at the other end. This continuum of gendered violence is used in civil society and in the home to remind women that they
do not belong as citizens and are always at risk (of violence, of murder, of
starvation, of financial insecurity, etc.).

Challenging Exclusionary Inclusion

Sikh Women, Religious Community,
and Devotional Acts

When asked about women's place in Sikhism, Hardev Singh Saini, a forty-three-year-old Scheduled Caste man, points to women's participation in all-female devotional organizations, Sukhmani Seva Societies,[1] as a manifestation of gender equality:

> Now women are active. Like in our colony, a Sukhmani Seva Society has been created by women; so a majority of the time when there is Sukhmani Sahib prayers in someone's home, women usually conduct these prayers. The *granthi* [priest] doesn't do it; the women do.

For Saini, the creation of all-women's Sukhmani Seva Societies demonstrates that Sikh women enjoy equality in religious life. Most research participants in this study, like many political science and Sikh studies scholars, assume that women's presence in formal institutions is evidence of women's equality. However, what these participants and scholars often overlook is the fact that even when formal institutions guarantee equality, individuals experience exclusionary inclusion at the local level.

Some point to Sikh women's participation in Sukhmani Seva Societies as a manifestation of women's equal role in religious life. I examine women's participation in devotional organizations to demonstrate how Sikh women both uphold and resist exclusionary inclusion in religious community. Sikh women often struggle to escape contradictory and conflicting gendered norms—women's religiosity, women's rights and duties, and women's purity and pollution—that essentialize women as inferior, polluted, and suspect. Yet, for some women membership in Sukhmani Seva Societies is an unexpected resource for active citizenship, where they reinforce and resist socially prescribed gender roles and discriminatory gender norms that cause their unequal belonging. These women enact their citizenship rights through their religious affiliation. A situated analysis of women's participation in Sukhmani Seva Societies opens up the possibility for understanding acts of devotion as acts of citizenship, thus upending longstanding assumptions about strong religious, communal, and kinship ties as antithetical to modern citizenship.

An ethnographic analysis of Sikh women's citizenship also provides a possible way forward when it comes to the current tensions between state, community, and gender in India. Without explicitly engaging these intellectual and political debates, Sikh women active in devotional organizations envision and enact more egalitarian interpersonal and community relations that understand gender equality and minority rights not as competing, but as coexisting. In doing so, these women open up the possibility of securing more egalitarian gender relations within religious communities.

By situating Sikh women's citizenship, this analysis also highlights the tension between mainstream understandings of religion as oppressive and religious women's varied and complex experience of religious life.[2] Such an analysis contributes to a growing literature on citizenship, agency, and devotional organizations across faith communities (Mahmood 2005; Banerjee 2005, 2006; Isin and Ustundag 2008; Menon 2010; Bilge 2010; Isin 2011; Ikegame 2012; Banerjee-Patel and Robinson 2017). Many of these scholars focus on citizen's everyday lived experience as members of devotional organizations to complicate traditional understandings of agency

(Bracke 2003; Bucar 2010; Parashar 2010; Burke 2012). Some scholars force a rethinking of citizenship by asking "how people enact citizenship through 'acts' of citizenship that invent new ways of becoming . . . citizens" (Isin 2012, 568; see also Neveu 2015). Still others turn to women's participation in devotional organizations to challenge simplistic, orientalizing understandings of women's agency (Mahmood 2005; Isin and Ustundag 2008; Isin 2011; Rinaldo 2014).

Scholars such as Sirma Bilge (2010, 24) put intersectionality studies in conversation with scholarship on women's religious agency to "push intersectionality scholarship into new theoretical grounds; where it should systematically attend to the religious/secular divide, which is rarely integrated to the collection of social divisions (gender, race, class) typically taken into account." Similarly, Jakeet Singh (2015, 670–671) engages scholarship on women's religious agency to challenge intersectionality scholarship "to consider an axis of difference that has received relatively little attention within its framework" because an attentiveness to religion can, in turn, open up "diverse notions and practices of both oppression and liberation." This chapter contributes to both literatures—women's religious agency and intersectionality—by centering religion as well as other forms of intersecting differences, by being attentive to a range of women's agency,[3] and by making visible the work of building contingent coalitions and solidarities across situated and embodied power differentials.

Looking at women's participation in devotional organizations enables an exploration of the following questions: How do Sikh women survive and navigate sexism in a community that denies its very existence? How do participants take action in a religious community that is committed to gender equality yet maintains gender-based exclusion and violence? Do Sikh women experience devotional organizations as sites of liberatory politics? Are Sikh women able to move beyond prescribed gender roles and identities through their participation in Sukhmani Seva Societies?

I argue that Sikh women often struggle to take political action because they are unable to escape contradictory and conflicting gendered norms— (1) women's religiosity, (2) women's rights and duties, and (3) women's purity—that essentialize women as inferior, polluted, and suspect. Sikh

women are simultaneously governed by gendered norms that are, by definition, in tension with one another, and therefore women will *consistently*
and *constantly* fall short because of the contradictory nature of these gendered norms. I also demonstrate how Sikh women simultaneously maintain and challenge exclusionary inclusion by, at times, challenging gender
roles, and, at other times, enacting these very gender norms.[4]

I also argue that women *sevadars* (volunteers or servants) understand
liberation as both *mukti* (spiritual liberation) and gender-based liberation.
For women active in Sukhmani Seva Societies these two goals—spiritual
and gender liberation—are inextricably linked in their struggle to open
public religious life to women so they can achieve their ultimate goal,
mukti—a place of honor at Vahiguru's feet. A situated analysis of citizenship does not assume a singular definition of liberation; rather it enables a
cogenerated understanding of the concept. Similarly, a situated analysis of
citizenship does not assume that gender equality is tied to secularization;
rather it leaves open the possibility of achieving gender justice in both secular and religious spaces. By doing so, this analysis makes visible how two
distinct definitions of liberation—political and religious—operate among
Sikh women, how these two seemingly unrelated goals are contingently
aligned, and how linking these two types of liberation can lead to more
egalitarian relations within religious communities.

I explain how and why women struggle to take political action because
they understand their own behavior, judge one another's behavior, and are
judged by community members through contradictory and conflicting
gendered norms that are, at times, explicit and, at other times, implicit.
I examine the interplay and tension between and within Sikh women's
multiple identities as they navigate and negotiate exclusionary inclusion.
By doing so, I make visible an uneven gendered experience of religious
community. I explore how women are split apart by differences, and how
they overcome these differences. I illustrate the process through which
women come to see themselves as public figures who serve Vahiguru and
community. I also demonstrate how some women expand prescribed
gender roles through access to public religious space in the face of exclusionary inclusion.

Sukhmani Seva Societies rarely engage the formal institutions of politics, such as elections, campaigns, and party politics.[5] As a result, it is easy to ignore the political character of these women's actions and to instead see them as religious, apolitical, civic, and charitable. This would be a mistake. Sukhmani Seva Societies also rarely engage in overtly feminist struggles, such as the debate surrounding a Uniform Civil Code and gender-based quotas or reservations (chapter 3). As a consequence, it is easy to overlook the liberatory nature of these women's actions and to instead see them as religious, traditional, customary, and antifeminist. Again, this would be a mistake. What is required is a more expansive definition of the political to understand that religious affiliations are not necessarily an obstacle to citizenship, but rather a way of enacting citizenship in a liberal democracy. What is also required is a rethinking of our conventional understanding of the feminist subject to understand that gender equality is not antithetical to religiosity, but rather religiosity can be a means for attaining political and religious liberation.

This analysis makes women's diverse political action visible and legible. On the one hand, some women challenge conflicting and contradictory gendered norms and, on the other hand, these very women express and enact the very norms that give rise to women's exclusion. On the one hand, some women open up public space for themselves and for others and, on the other hand, these very women limit women's access to public space by policing women's inclusion. On the one hand, some women fight for freedom from male domination and, on the other hand, these very women internalize male domination.

In the following section, I provide a detailed discussion of Sukhmani Seva Societies. Next, I discuss interview and participant observation findings, with attention to the ways participants (1) essentialize women as inferior, polluted, and suspect through contradictory and conflicting gender norms; (2) enact citizenship through acts of devotion; and (3) engage in democratic practice rooted in Guru's grace to survive and perhaps thrive in the face of exclusionary inclusion. I conclude by discussing the implications of my findings for gender, citizenship, and democracy in the Sikh community and beyond.

SUKHMANI SEVA SOCIETIES

Sukhmani Seva Societies,[6] also referred to as Sukhmani Sahib Seva (or Sewa) Societies, are devotional religious organizations open to men and women that promote the recitation of Sukhmani Sahib prayers at a grassroots level in Punjab and throughout India.[7] The recitation of Sukhmani Sahib has a long history, but the rise of Sukhmani Seva Societies is a relatively recent phenomenon.[8]

Sukhmani Seva Societies tend to be active in religious, civic, and charitable service. For example, these devotional organizations often provide religious functions, such as *langar* (communal kitchen), *kirtan* (congregational singing of hymns), *nagar kirtan* (processional singing of hymns), and *chhabeel* (communal sweetened water).[9] They also provide civic and public services, such as medical services, infrastructure improvements, and social assistance. For example, in 2000 in Abohar, Punjab, a road crossing popularly known as "killer *chowk* [road crossing]" was renamed Sri Sukhmani Seva Society Chowk after the devotional organization paid for infrastructure repairs. In 2001 in Bathinda, Punjab, a Sukhmani Seva Society organized a hepatitis B vaccination camp.

Sukhmani Seva Societies' primary objective is *seva* (service) to their community and propagation of Sikh faith. These organizations value their autonomy and are not directly affiliated with the Shiromani Gurdwara Prabandhak Committee (SGPC).[10] Also, there is no singular hierarchical organizing structure that governs all Sukhmani Seva Societies. These societies are highly autonomous and localized. The service activities of Sukhmani Seva Societies are most often tied to local *gurdwaras* (Sikh temples).[11]

In the following sections, I focus attention on how Sikh women negotiate the terms of religious and civic participation in three interrelated sites—Sukhmani Sevi Societies, *gurdwaras*, and home. I select the interplay between these three sites because women's participation in these sites can contribute to the development of neighborhoods, provide public services, cultivate religious, political, and civic identities, and build communities and solidarities.

GENDERED NORMS AND UNEVEN ACCESS
TO RELIGIOUS COMMUNITY

In this section, I analyze semi-structured, in-depth interview data with women who are active in Sukhmani Seva Societies to demonstrate that women are governed by contradictory and conflicting gender norms resulting in their unequal access to religious community. I find three kinds of gendered norms that contribute to exclusionary inclusion: (1) women's religiosity, (2) women's rights and duties, and (3) women's purity. These norms create a situation where women are never fully included; essentialized as inferior, polluted, and suspect; and constrained in their ability to take political, civic, and religious action.

I focus on the interview responses of three women, who are founding members and active *sevadars* in their local Sukhmani Seva Societies: Hardeep Kaur Bedi, a fifty-five-year-old Khatri woman, Harsimran Kaur Sagoo, a sixty-one-year-old Ramgarhia woman, and Rupinder Kaur, a sixty-two-year-old Khatri woman. Bedi is an *amritdhari* Sikh (most traditionally religious) who completed a master's degree in Punjabi and is a housewife. Sagoo is a *kesdhari* Sikh (more moderately religious) who completed twelfth grade and is a housewife. Kaur is an *amritdhari* Sikh (most traditionally religious) who completed twelfth grade and is a retired teacher. This information helps to complicate often simplistic characterizations of devout women as predominantly orthodox and uneducated.

When I asked female research participants about their participation in civic and associational life, their responses, unlike male participants, were centered on the home (chapter 4). Given most women's responses regarding civic and associational life, I was surprised to learn that Bedi, Sagoo, and Kaur are founding members of their respective devotional organizations. Bedi is a founding member and first president of Mata Khivi[12] Sukhmani Seva Society, and Sagoo and Kaur are founding members of Mata Gujri[13] Sukhmani Seva Society. Both societies are named in honor of revered Sikh women from the Guru period, who helped to found the very institutions and practices that guarantee equality in the Sikh community.

Women *sevadars* experienced religious community as uneven. On the one hand, women *sevadars* experienced religious community as a hostile and, at times, violent space. They were repeatedly denied access to public religious life. On the other hand, these women actively participated in religious life and radically altered their communities by transforming nearly defunct *gurdwaras* into vibrant devotional and public spaces. These *sevadars* also participated in a network of local all-female Sukhmani Seva Societies and inspired other women to create devotional organizations. Even as these women expanded traditional gender roles and challenged some gender norms, they simultaneously maintained other gendered norms and policed women's bodies in the private space of the home and in the public religious space of the *gurdwara*.

Women's Religiosity

According to many research participants, women's religiosity determines their access to the three key elements of citizenship: rights and duties, belonging, and membership (chapter 4). According to these participants, women's adherence to *bani* (the word of God) and *bana* (religious dress) determines their belonging in the community. Fateh Singh, a forty-two-year-old Ramgarhia man, who is a *granthi* (custodian of *gurdwara* and caretaker and reader of the Guru Granth) with a primary school education, conceives of women's citizenship rights as contingent upon their religiosity:

The mistreatment of women in the Sikh community is caused by a deficiency in one's commitment to the *bani*. . . . Before [the Guru period] women did not have religious freedom; Guru Nanak Sahib gave this religious freedom to women. But I will not hesitate to say that even though Guru Nanak gave women religious freedom, most women have not used this freedom in a proper way. Women haven't used this freedom in a proper way! Women use this freedom to pursue their own pleasures. Some women use freedom to pursue what is financially beneficial. . . . Other women use their freedom to pursue fashion. Some have gone so far as to forgo their own bodily modesty and respect. . . . When people have knowledge of Sikhism, then there will be respect of women.

According to Fateh Singh, women are responsible for their own mistreatment because of their incomplete adoption of Sikhism. Singh articulates a Sikh narrative of egalitarianism, which portrays (1) women as unequal prior to Sikhism, (2) Sikhism as securing and enshrining gender equality, and (3) gender inequality as a failure to fully adopt Sikhism (chapter 4). Singh claims that women are not using their religious freedom as dictated by *bani*, but are using it for financial gain and pursuit of fashion, thus forgoing their own bodily modesty and respect. In short, Singh explains sexism as an incomplete adoption of Sikhism. By doing so, Singh frees himself and others of any responsibility for sexist practices and shifts blame to women whose commitment to *bani* is defined as deficient and whose religiosity is always suspect. In doing so, Fateh Singh elevates religious purity over gender equality.

Fateh Singh's response is significant because of his formal role as *granthi* of a local *gurdwara*. Singh enjoys some degree of power, influence, and prestige within the *gurdwara* and local community. This power is limited because often *granthis*, like Fateh Singh, come from scheduled-caste backgrounds and use the position of *granthi* to uplift themselves and their families from poverty and caste-based stigma. Nonetheless, given that all-female devotional organizations locate their devotional lives and practices in local *gurdwaras*, *granthis* like Fateh Singh have significant power to limit these women's access to local *gurdwaras*, characterize their devotion as a threat to male power and material security, and essentialize them as religiously suspect. Furthermore, *granthis* also enjoy significant power to teach others about informal rules and unwritten norms that naturalize women's inferior position and results in their second-class citizenship.

Fateh Singh's response is also representative of the fact that Sikh women find themselves in a contradictory situation where they will, by definition, always fail to meet gendered norms and fulfill gender roles. For example, the gendered norm of women's right and duties, which defines women's role in relation to marriage and limits women's participation to the home, is in tension with the gendered norm of women's religiosity, which defines women's rights and duties as contingent upon their religiosity and requires engagement with Sikh institutions outside the home. According to the norm of women's religiosity, women are assumed to be religiously suspect and deficient and must prove their religiosity. According to the norm of women's rights and duties, women are defined as mothers and wives in service to home and marriage.

But how can women be sufficiently religious when expectations about appropriate gender roles limit women's participation to the private space of the home? How can women be religiously devout when pursuing that devotion requires participation and membership beyond home and marriage? As discussed below, when women pursue their religious devotion as *sevadars* in Sukhmani Seva Societies, they are often characterized as inadequate mothers, wives, and daughters in-law. Women find themselves in a double bind in which their commitment to their religiosity makes them inadequate mothers and wives, and their commitment to their home and marriage makes them insufficiently religious.

These contradictory and competing norms make it impossible for women to fully belong in either the private space of the home or in the public religious space of the *gurdwara*. These implicit gendered norms also constrain women's political action, religious activity, and civic engagement, and create incomplete access to religious community.

Women's Rights and Duties

Most participants understand women as partial members of their communities with limited rights and duties, which center primarily on the private space of the home defined in relation to men and marriage (chapter 4). *Sevadars* who were actively pursuing religious devotion vis-à-vis Sukhmani Seva Societies often expressed this particular gendered norm.

Bedi explains that when she started the Sukhmani Seva Society, she came up against many difficulties as its first president:

> At that point, my children were all unmarried, and I started a weekly program, every Thursday. And I was the first president of the Sukhmani Seva Society. In the beginning, I came up against many, many difficulties because all of the ladies would say to me, "Your daughters are old enough to do household work when you are away, but we have young, young children. How will we manage?" I would then plead with them, "You tell me what time works for you, and we will do it at that time." For six months, we couldn't even come up with a day of the week. Should we do it on Thursday or Wednesday? Because some people raised havoc if we suggested one day, and others got upset if you suggested the other.

Bedi was singled out by the other *sevadars* because Bedi's daughters were older, and therefore they could share in household work. This gave Bedi some flexibility that others did not enjoy. Bedi struggled to build solidarity with the other women because her daughters were unmarried and could temporarily contribute to the household duties, relieving some of her burdens. The other women, however, had younger daughters who could not take on household duties. This difference between the ages of female children led to intense negotiation amongst *sevadars* and created some animosity between them. The tensions between household duties and religious devotion made it more difficult to build solidarity and trust among *sevadars*.

Bedi and her fellow *sevadars* also struggled for six months to determine a day to meet. The women struggled to find a suitable day to express their religious devotion because there was *no* day of the week when these women were free of their rights and duties as mother's and wives. The women's attempt at organizing was made more difficult because they are navigating possible participation in a devotional organization while expressing an understanding of women as restricted to home and marriage. In navigating these gender roles, women often find themselves in a double bind where they are judged by others and often judge one another based on conflicting gender norms that are impossible to live up to. The women's desire to be *good* mothers, wives, and daughters in-law who care for their children, complete their household responsibilities, and serve their husbands and in-laws is in tension with their desire for religious devotion, which requires them to leave the home and be active in their local *gurdwaras* as *sevadars* of Vahiguru and *sangat* (congregation). The women struggled to build solidarity and trust because they were torn between religious devotion and women's rights and duties.

Women who fail to meet prescribed gender roles may find themselves subjected to a continuum of gendered violence, from emotional violence to physical assault. Women who fail to meet expectations may become the subject of rumor, ridicule, and gossip in the home and in the community. Women may also experience more extreme forms of violence like domestic violence, sexual assault, stalking, and groping in the home and in the community.

When explaining the difficulties associated with maintaining Sukhmani Seva Societies, Sagoo, a founding member of Mata Gujri Sukhmani Seva Society, also discusses the limited time and resources available to women because of their household duties. When asked how often she went to the *gurdwara*, Sagoo replies:

> We do our weekly *kirtan* at the village *gurdwara*. The *seva* I partake in is mostly reading of the scripture. I only have enough time to do this. You know, ladies have limited time. We start prayers at 10:00 a.m., and by 12:00 or 12:30 we complete our prayers. Then after that we come home and take care of work around the house.

Sagoo, like Bedi, discusses the difficulty associated with balancing household responsibilities with religious devotion. Both women identify the tension between their devotion, which requires them to enter public space, and women's rights and duties, which require them to stay within the private space of the home fulfilling gendered familial duties. An ethnographic analysis of women's participation in Sukhmani Seva Societies shows that women are conflicted and torn about their understanding of themselves and their understanding of one another as mothers and wives and as devout *sevadars*. An analysis of Sikh women's material and embodied situatedness illuminates the fact that implicit gendered norms constrain women's political action and civic engagement at multiple levels—individual, organizational, and communal.

However, in the face of contradictory and conflicting gender norms, Bedi, Sagoo, and their fellow *sevadars* open up a new role for themselves, a role separate from the private space of the home within the public space of the *gurdwara*. In the face of exclusionary inclusion, they are able to take political action even if these actions are not immediately recognizable as political. Through religious devotion, some Sikh women are able to actively engage in religious community independently of (and perhaps at the cost of) their domestic responsibilities. Religious devotion enables these women to navigate, negotiate, and challenge gender roles, at times expanding women's access beyond the home, thus challenging norms that construct the home as the natural space of Sikh women.

Sikh women come to identify as Sikh by navigating between multiple and contradictory identities. Sikh women do not easily or simply identify as Sikh; they do not automatically see themselves and each other as *sevadars* devoted to Vahiguru and *sangat*. Rather Sikh women struggle to forge this identity for themselves and for their organization as they navigate and negotiate between public religious participation and socially prescribed familial roles and the burdens of domestic duties.

Women's Purity and Pollution

Many female participants, including some members of devotional organizations, understand women as partial members of the Sikh community with limited rights and duties because of the logic of purity and pollution (chapter 4). I was surprised that women who were active in Sukhmani Seva Societies held these views. These women were highly versed in Sikh scripture and code of conduct, which explicitly denounce women's impurity and pollution associated with reproduction. They recited from memory Guru Nanak's hymn challenging women's pollution—"Then why call her inferior/polluted from whom, / All great ones [rajas] are born" (Guru Granth, 473)? Yet some of these women expressed notions of purity and pollution.

For example, Bedi expresses multiple, conflicting gender norms simultaneously. At times, she adheres to religious devotion to open public spaces to women, while, at other times, she espouses an unwritten implicit rule regarding women's purity and pollution, which functions to justify discrimination against women:

> Women aren't allowed in that particular position as a *granthi*, but we still have access to the Guru Granth sahib. We go to the guru's home and sit before the Guru Granth; we have the Granth sahib in our homes; and we can pray in the *gurdwara*. For instance, when we start a prayer, we go to the *gurdwara*, and we recite from Guru Granth sahib for two hours at a time. We sit before the Guru Granth sahib, in the same place that the *granthi* sits. There is no restriction per se. But it is the case that we are in a male-dominated country, and we ourselves give in to male domination. There is also a separate issue; there is one more issue. Women are not pure for some time due to a God-given trait. Women can achieve the highest of high levels, but ultimately we remain part of the female race. On a natural basis, we can't always partake in and maintain our duties to our *seva*.

Bedi describes women's access to and relationship with the Granth as restricted and qualified. After outlining the ways in which women are equal to male *granthis* and enjoy access to the scripture unmediated by male authority, Bedi points to the differences.

According to Bedi, there are two prominent differences between male *granthis* and female *sevadars*: (1) women must contend with a male-dominated country; and (2) women suffer from impurity and pollution associated with menstruation and childbirth. Male domination, for Bedi, partially explains women's limited access to the public space of the *gurdwara* and the Granth. Bedi identifies male domination in the Indian nation as one of the causes of gender-based discrimination in the Sikh community. Bedi adopts a narrative of Sikh exceptionalism and points to male domination as a national problem that exists elsewhere, in other communities, not among Sikhs. For Bedi, the Sikh community's egalitarian principles are tainted by India's problem with misogyny and patriarchy. Bedi's response demonstrates how minority Sikh women use gender to express solidarity with their minority religious communities while distancing themselves from the Indian state often equated with Hindu hegemony and propagation of sexism and casteism. Bedi also identifies women's internalization of male domination as a cause for gender-based discrimination in the Sikh community. She argues that Sikh women themselves give in to male domination by internalizing female subordination and adopting socially prescribed gender roles.

After discussing male domination, Bedi points to the logic of embodied purity and pollution to explain differential treatment of women in the Sikh community. Bedi's statement that "on a natural basis, [women] can't always partake in and maintain our duties to our *seva*" makes sense if one assumes, first, that menstruation and childbirth cause pollution and, second, that those who are polluted should not touch or be near the Guru Granth. According to norms of purity and pollution, women must accept the fact that they cannot be *granthis* because biologically they are impure, which means they cannot conduct religious functions, such as reading scripture, singing *kirtan*, and distributing *prasad*. While Bedi pushes back at the conventional definition of women's role by expanding women's access to public religious life, she simultaneously restricts women's power in the *gurdwara* by adopting a gendered norm of purity and pollution, which, in turn, legitimizes women's exclusion.

Rupinder Kaur, a founding member of the Mata Gujri Sukhmani Seva Societies, explains how women learn about implicit gendered norms:

We [Sikh women] come to know these things [regarding purity and pollution] within our family; our mother, *bhua* [paternal aunt], *masi* [maternal aunt] . . . would tell us at this time, "You don't go to the *gurdwara*, at this time you don't bow before Guru Granth." All of this is taught within the family.

Older women actively police younger women's behavior and action by teaching them about implicit, unwritten rules, like purity and pollution, that contradict Sikh scripture and code of conduct, and result in women's exclusion. Mothers, *bhuas*, and *masis* teach girls about informal and unspoken rules in the private space of the home, which, in turn, normalize women's inferiority and exclusion in the religious community.

In a single interview response, Bedi explains gender discrimination in *gurdwaras* by shifting blame to majority group domination and shifting responsibility to female reproduction and biology. On the one hand, Bedi links the goal of gender equality with minority group autonomy when she locates the problem of discrimination with Hindu domination. On the other hand, Bedi adopts the gendered norm of purity and pollution, which limits women's belonging and membership in the home and in the religious community. Bedi's interview response challenges any simplistic understanding of women's participation in devotional organizations as wholly democratic or nondemocratic or as solely progressive or regressive. Rather, an analysis of her interview responses makes visible a complex understanding and experience of gender identities and interests, where Sikh women simultaneously challenge exclusionary inclusion through religious devotion and naturalize exclusionary inclusion through purity and pollution.

A situated, ethnographic analysis of Sikh women's devotion shows that identities and interests are lived as complicated, contradictory, and fragmentary, and therefore a "pre-ordained link" (Lee 2008) between identity and politics cannot be assumed. At times, Sikh women envision and enact egalitarian gender relations that understand gender equality and minority rights as coexisting. However, at other times, Sikh women uphold exclusionary inclusion by maintaining gendered norms that constrain women's political action and religious practice at the individual, organizational, and community level.

CHALLENGING EXCLUSIONARY INCLUSION

In this section, I continue the analysis of ethnographic data cogenerated with Hardeep Kaur Bedi, Harsimran Kaur Sagoo, and Rupinder Kaur. This analysis makes visible certain forms of citizenship that have been systematically ignored because strong religious, communal, and kinship ties are often seen as antithetical to democratic inclusion and citizenship practice (chapter 2). Rather than assuming that religious affiliations are an obstacle to citizenship, I show how religious affiliations might be a way of enacting citizenship in India. This analysis also makes visible religious women's varied and complex agency, which is often overlooked because these women are assumed to be willing participants in their own subordination. Rather than assuming that religious community is experienced as either wholly empowering or disempowering, I show how within a single religious community there are diverse understandings of both subordination and liberation. Through an embodied, situated analysis of women's participation in Sukhmani Seva Societies, I reveal (1) how acts of devotion can be understood as acts of citizenship in a liberal democracy; (2) how the identity category and subject position of woman *sevadar* is forged; and (3) how religious space can be conducive to more egalitarian gender relations that envision gender equality and minority rights as linked goals.

Acts of Devotion as Citizenship Acts

When asked about their participation in devotional organizations, both Bedi and Sagoo describe in detail the lack of Sikh religious services and life in their particular village. According to Bedi:

> In the beginning, when this *gurdwara* was first made, it opened once every month. The *pathi* [keeper of the *granth*] would also say that the *gurdwara* would open in a month. However, once we established our Sukhmani Seva Society, we made a *kirtani jatha* [organization for devotional singing]. We did this because this is a Hindu village and

people; therefore, most engage in "Jai Mataji, Jai Mataji" [hail the divine Mother]. . . . When the ladies from my street would say, "We are having [Hindu] *kirtan* at our home; you must come," I would go, but on a social basis. I would sit among them socially. I went thinking, "Okay, if I don't attend their function, then tomorrow if I have an event or function, they won't attend, either." So I would go but on a social basis. I would sit down among them, but my mind was constantly saying, "Vahiguru, Vahiguru." And I would say to myself, "I wish that we too would have some type of weekly function like this."

Bedi expresses her longing for a vibrant Sikh community in a village where Sikh religious life was absent. This longing motivates Bedi and her fellow female *sevadars* to intervene in *gurdwara* life, which had been under male supervision and guidance, and transform it from monthly services to weekly services under all-female leadership. Bedi recalls the experience of attending Hindu *kirtan*, reciting "Jai Mataji, Jai Mataji," while in her mind reciting "Vahiguru, Vahiguru," and envisioning an active community of Sikh devotees. Bedi explains that her *ardas*, her petition, to hear "Vahiguru, Vahiguru" throughout her village was heard:

This village is a Hindu village, it's traditionally a Hindu location. But I from early on have had a deep love for Guru Nanak Devji and I would say, "Maharaj, we should hear 'Vahiguru, Vahiguru' throughout the village." And now that it has happened, I am very pleased.

Bedi is pleased that, with Guru Nanak Devji's grace, she and her Sukhmani Seva Society actualized her vision by ensuring that "Vahiguru, Vahiguru" is heard alongside "Jai Mataji, Jai Mataji" in their respective religious spaces in a Hindu dominant village.

Bedi and her fellow *sevadars* link gender equality with minority group autonomy while preserving religious pluralism. They create a vibrant devotional community that values women's leadership, religiosity, and equality. They create a harmonious relationship between the minority

Sikh community and the majority Hindu village. For Bedi, Sikh and Hindu *kirtan* should be sung alongside one another; villagers should hear chants of both "Vahiguru" and "Mataji" throughout the village. Bedi and the others actualized a vision rooted in religious pluralism where active Sikh devotees coexist in harmony with members of the majority Hindu community.

Bedi explains that, with Guru Nanak Devji's grace, the devotional organization successfully impacted citizens in her village and in neighboring villages:

> We have weekly functions, we have a yearly function commemorating the start of our Sukhmani Seva Society, we are given *saropas* [honorary lengths of cloth].[14] And now if you look at it, in every home there is a woman affiliated with the Sukhmani Society, and in every home people are taking Maharaj's name. And in our neighboring villages, women have followed our lead and they have established Sukhmani Seva Societies too. When we have functions here, for example if we celebrate Guru Nanak's birthday or Guru Gobind's birthday, the women from the neighboring villages come to our events to honor us and they present us with *saropas*. God's grace is with us at the moment. Everyone is shocked that such a small organization like ours has been able to last. At the moment, we have anywhere from twenty-five to thirty members. It doesn't matter if one member is gone here and if another member is gone there. Every week at least five, seven, or ten women are present. And if we are going to have any main programs, then we are all present. And in addition to that, we have the *sangat* [congregation] of the village. I am so joyous that at least I can say that I have been born into this world and I have done at least one good deed.

Bedi and her fellow *sevadars* created a vibrant organization of thirty members who are supported by their local *sangat* and are highly active in all levels of service—weekly reading of scripture and singing of *kirtan*, yearly commemoration of gurus' births, and yearly commemoration of their devotional organizations. These women influenced *all* homes in their own village and inspired women in other villages to establish their own Sukhmani Seva Societies. The very women who often essentialize one another and are essentialized by community members as inferior, polluted, and suspect see themselves and other female *sevadars* as integral members of their community worthy of public honor and blessed by God's grace. This is one example of how Sikh women created more egalitarian interpersonal and community relations through their participation in devotional organizations. This is one example of how Sikh women realized a vision of spiritual liberation and gender liberation as joint goals.

Like Bedi, Sagoo also finds religious activity at her local *gurdwara* lacking:

> Yes, actually I started the Sukhmani Seva Society when I moved here. I started it. See, when I first came here, at that time, nothing was done in the *gurdwara*. There was no *kirtan*—nothing at all. There weren't even any gents who conducted *kirtan*. There was one gentleman—at least as far as I know—there was one blind gentleman, a poor man who didn't read *gurbani*. He would sing songs, for example, religious songs. He is the only one who did anything at the *gurdwara*. Then one day, I sang a *shabad* [devotional song], and afterward some of the people of the village came to me and suggested that I start an *istri satsang* [women's devotional association]. Then I started it here.

Sagoo describes her longing to express her religious devotion and build a vibrant community of Sikh devotees. She identifies this desire as her and her fellow *sevadars'* motivation for starting an *istri satsang*, which transformed *gurdwara* life under all-female leadership. Sagoo and her fellow female *sevadars* are fulfilling their religious devotion while meeting the religious needs of the community, a need not filled by the "gents."

What I am suggesting is that we consider Bedi's and Sagoo's devotional acts as citizenship acts, which contribute to the development of their communities, provide public goods and services to their communities, and function as an infrastructure of civic, religious, and political interaction.

Both women contribute to their communities by radically transforming nearly defunct *gurdwaras* into vibrant devotional and public spaces. They also create a network of local women's Sukhmani Seva Societies that travel to neighboring villages serving Vahiguru and *sangat*. By doing so, Bedi and Sagoo open up the possibility of significant transformation of gender norms and roles by entering civic and associational life, exercising their freedom of association and travel, and placing women in a position of honor at the center of devotional life.

Bedi and Sagoo created vibrant, active *gurdwaras*, which provide religious, civic, and public services to their respective communities. They cultivated complicated and contradictory civic, religious, and political identities, and articulated complicated and contradictory solidarities as citizens. Participation in devotional organizations is one way Sikh women enact their citizenship rights, but these acts are often overlooked and ignored as religious and apolitical or oppressive and antifeminist. An examination of Sikh women's situated citizenship forces a rethinking of conventional understandings of religious community in India by demonstrating that the religious sphere can be a space of democratic participation and inclusion, especially in the face of exclusionary inclusion. This analysis suggests that for some Sikh women religious community can be a potential site from which to challenge exclusionary inclusion and negotiate between state, community, and gender in new ways.

Overcoming External and Internal Divisions through the Guru's Grace

Bedi describes the public skepticism and mocking that Mata Khivi members faced when they entered public religious life, and how they overcame it through the guru's grace:

> And then at that point, other big-big [high-status] men in the village said, "These women have just started organizing; they won't last two months." Then I got all the women together and said to

them, . . . "Look, the entire village has challenged us. They say that we won't last." And we then made an *ardas* [petition or prayer closing congregational worship] to Guru Nanak. We said, "We want to come together in your name. We want to follow your path. Please ensure that we keep walking on your path." And today we have been active now for ten years.

For Bedi, a turning point came when their organizing was publicly challenged and mocked by high-status men. This public mocking prompted individual and collective action through religious devotion. Bedi explains that the women came together through *ardas*, in which they made a communal plea to follow Nanak's path through their devotional organization, and now they have been active for ten years.

Bedi does not attribute the group's success to her leadership, to the group's resources, to an opportune moment, or to any other such factor. For Bedi, her and her fellow *sevadars* are only partially responsible for their own actions, and many of their accomplishments are attributed to divine agency. Bedi does not engage in direct confrontation with those who publicly mocked her and her fellow *sevadars*. Rather Bedi and Mata Khivi members respond through collective devotion and submission. In short, for Bedi, their organization has been able to serve Vahiguru and the *sangat* for ten years because their communal *ardas* was fulfilled by the guru's grace.

Sagoo also encounters public skepticism and mocking based on the gender of the Mata Gujri members, and similarly, she attributes the group's success to the guru's grace:

When I first started, I actually encountered a lot of problems. Some people said, "This organization will never function." Some people said, "How will you ladies be able to do this? You won't be able to do it." I am not sure why people said these things. I don't know if they said it because we are ladies. But Maharaj's [God's] grace was with us, and I can guarantee that now the organization can't be stopped. When we started there were only two or three ladies. Even at the moment there aren't that many of us. There are many Radhasoamis [members of religious communities of guru bhaktis or devotees to a living guru][15] who are part of our group. Otherwise there are only two or three of us [non-Radhasoami Sikh women]. Maharaj's grace has been with us.

For Sagoo, the women are able to establish and maintain a devotional organization that she characterizes as unstoppable because God's grace is with them. Sagoo and the Mata Gujri members do not directly confront those who questioned their capacity to organize. Rather, they respond through collective devotion and submission. Sagoo attributes the success of her local Sukhmani Seva Society not to any one individual, to any particular characteristic of the group, or to a particularly opportune moment. Rather, she explains the success through divine agency and Maharaj's grace. Sagoo, like Bedi, experienced the religious community as hostile, discriminatory, and violent. Yet, with the guru's grace these women entered public religious life and created a space to express their religious devotion.

Sagoo and Kaur, both founding members of the Mata Gujri Sukhmani Seva Society, explain that Vahiguru enabled the women to overcome not only external obstacles, but also internal divisions. In particular, they explain that initially the group was divided based on religious belief, as some women identified as Sikh and others identified as Radhasoami.[16] Rupinder Kaur describes the internal religious divisions in the following way:

Yes, when we started [Sukhmani Seva Society] we did encounter some difficulties. The beliefs of the people in this village didn't match with our beliefs. These same women are now sitting with us, and slowly over time we have grown to love one another. These women cooperate so much with us, to the point that now our society can't function without them. Now these same women have developed the positive habit of *naam japna* [meditation or chanting of "Vahiguru"]. And therefore, now we can't function without them. Initially, there were religious differences between us. These people, some of them,

didn't believe in pure *gursikhi* [Sikhism]. These people to some degree were more inclined toward Radhasoami. Otherwise, these
women have never objected to us. They have learned such beautiful
kirtan. Now they have learned such beautiful *kirtan*. It makes my
heart happy. In the beginning, however, there was some difficulty
surrounding this issue.

Kaur explains that the Radhasoami women's devotion to a living guru
was in tension with Sikh women's submission to Vahiguru. According to
Kaur and Sagoo, this tension was overcome and love and cooperation was
fostered between the two groups through Sikh religious practice of *naam
japna, prasad*, and *kirtan*. This particular Sikh devotional organization,
the Mata Gujri Sukhmani Seva Society, is composed primarily of non-
Sikhs, composed primarily of Radhasoamis, yet it is functioning as an unstoppable Sikh devotional organization.

The fact that the Mata Gujri society is composed of both Sikhs and
Radhasoamis shows a tolerance for religious diversity within Sikh devotional organizations. Kaur's and Sagoo's interview responses also demonstrate that shared religious solidarity did not simply exist between the
women; rather this trust and solidarity was created through the work of
the Sukhmani Seva Society. Lastly, their interview responses demonstrate
how the women created an unstoppable organization and overcame external community skepticism and internal religious differences through
God's grace and through Sikh practices, not through direct confrontation
with authority or power.

Bedi also outlines internal divisions in the Mata Khivi devotional organ-
ization. When Bedi talks about organizing *all* the women in the village,
she is careful to explain the caste and class differences between the women.
She states that the other high-caste, Khatri women were reluctant to join
Bedi and the other *sevadars*, and they insisted that Bedi, a Khatri woman,
join them at the Hindu temple: "Then I got all the women together. . . .
And the Khatri women got angry with me. They would say, 'You are also
Khatri, so why aren't you going to the *mandir* [Hindu temple]?'" Bedi
describes how caste and class split the women apart as the upper-caste

women expected Bedi to organize based on *caste* not *religion* and, therefore, join them in the Hindu temple. Sagoo's, Kaur's, and Bedi's interview
responses demonstrate that there was no simple or easy identity category
from which to mobilize and organize. Rather, all three express how they
overcame caste, class, and religious difference to forge solidarity through
the identity category and subject position of women *sevadars*.

Negotiating Organizational Structure through Divine Agency

Sagoo explains the unique organizational structure of the Mata Gujri
Sukhmani Seva Society by pointing to divine agency:

> The name of our *jatha* [organized group of Sikhs with a religious or
> political mission] is Mata Gujriji. Mata Gujriji is the name of our
> *jatha*. The interesting thing about this particular *jatha*, about the
> women associated with this *jatha*, is the fact that among us there
> is no president, there is no secretary, there is no one like that. Our
> *sangat* [congregation] gets along beautifully; and our program
> has been going for four years now. And we come together every
> Thursday and we volunteer together. This is all I would like to say.
> The most interesting aspect is the fact that we don't have a president;
> we don't have any titles. In most cases, when you start any type of
> organization, this is the first difficulty you face, the first hurdle you
> face. But we don't have any of these issues. We are functioning under
> the title Mata Gujri's *satsang* [devotional association], that's it. . . .
> Vahiguru has created this uniqueness [of no internal hierarchy] in
> our organization.

Sukhmani Seva Societies are highly autonomous organizations that determine their own internal organizational structure, devotional practices, and
philanthropic services. An examination of these two organizations reveals
a high degree of variability when it comes to organizational structures.
Bedi describes herself as the founding president of the Sukhmani Seva

Society, whereas Sagoo explains that she is a founding member of an organization without titles. Sagoo supports an organization without presidents, without secretaries, and without titles because this reflects the egalitarian values of Sikhism. Again, Sagoo points to divine agency to explain the unique, nonhierarchical, and democratic character of the Mata Gujri devotional organization.

Prevailing understandings of religious communities in India assume that religious relations are nondemocratic, hierarchical, and oppressive; however, an ethnographic analysis of Sukhmani Seva Societies reveals that women's democratic participation and inclusion can occur in the very spaces assumed to be undemocratic. This analysis also reveals how Sikh women use mutual love, cooperation, and trust to overcome caste, class, and religious differences and forge the subject position of women *sevadars*. Sikh women experience Sukhmani Seva Societies not as wholly oppressive, but as uneven. Women through the guru's grace are empowered momentarily to be leaders, decision-makers, devotees, *granthis, pathis, kirtanis*, and *ragis*. And these very women simultaneously police women's bodies, judging themselves and each other based on oppressive gender norms and gender roles.

Bedi and Sagoo also discuss the initial internal and external suspicion of the women, especially as it relates to the *gurdwara's* finances. Bedi explains that the male *pathi* (reader of Guru Granth) was suspicious of her and her fellow *sevadars*:

Many people used to say to us, "With what motivation have you started this organization." At first, our *pathi* wouldn't let us enter the *gurdwara*. He would say to us, "You are going to take all of the gurdwara's *maya* [money or wealth]; you will take the money that is given to the *ragis* [musicians of *kirtan*]. People give ten or fifteen rupees to the *kirtani* [musicians] and when you add it all up, it can total six or seven hundred rupees. And some of our ladies even said, "Let's divide the money among ourselves." And I said wait a second, we have started this journey in the name of religion, and if we divide the money, then it's a business. So, I said, let's give the money to the *pathi*; that way he won't object to our organization. Now whenever the *pathi* goes to the *gurdwara* he says, in the speaker system and so and so's house, there will be a *sukhmani path*, and such and such place there will be a *sukhmani path*, all the ladies should attend. And then other people invite us to conduct prayers in their homes, and they ask, "What do you charge?" And we say, "We don't take anything, we don't charge anything."

The male *pathi* physically restricted Mata Khivi Sukhmani Seva Society members from entering the public space of the *gurdwara* because the *pathi* feared that the women would undermine his power, prestige, and financial security. To overcome this external suspicion, the women decided to donate all the money they collected from prayers and *kirtan* to the local *gurdwara*. By doing so, they were able to enter to the *gurdwara* and also transform their relationship with the *pathi* from adversary to ally. The women also faced an internal challenge as they decided how to shape the financial structure of their organization. Some women wanted to divide the money among organization members, but ultimately the group decided that all money should remain in the hands of the local *gurdwara*. Bedi explains that the society members "don't take anything; we don't charge anything."

Similarly, Sagoo describes internal suspicion regarding her intentions as it relates to *maya* collection:

We started the organization on September 16. Every year we celebrate the initiation of the organization by having prayers on the Thursday following September 16. . . . And then all of the *maya* that is collected we donate directly to the *gurdwara*. We don't give the money every day; we collect and give it to the *gurdwara* once a year after we celebrate our organization. We give it after a year, as much as we have collected. One or two ladies did say to me that I was going to keep the money and that I wouldn't donate it to the *gurdwara*. But generally speaking, this hasn't been a big problem for me. I don't think that anyone has truly been suspicious of me or accused me of anything.

Generally speaking, most of the money is with me until we donate it to the *gurdwara*. And from what I can tell no one has ever been worried about my intentions. And after a year goes by we give all of the money to the *gurdwara*.

Sagoo states that some members of the organization questioned her intentions and were suspicious that she would keep the money collected by the Sukhmani Seva Society. However, with time these suspicions appear to have subsided as the group members built trust and solidarity.

Each Sukhmani Seva Society is highly autonomous and determines its own rules as it relates to *maya* collection. Sagoo's organization waited an entire year before donating money to the local *gurdwara*, whereas Bedi's organization donated money to the local *gurdwara* immediately. This difference demonstrates the independence of the members who discuss, deliberate, and decide each aspect of the organizational structure from religious practice to financial structure.

In the face of inescapable, mutually conflicting gender norms, both Bedi and Sagoo identified a religious need and set out to fulfill this need. These women were animated by their religious devotion and directed by divine agency and the guru's grace, which enabled them to forge identities and solidarities as women *sevadars*, who entered the public space of the *gurdwara* and recited scripture and sang *kirtan*. A situated approach to citizenship opens up the possibility for seeing and understanding acts of submission as citizenship acts without overlooking them because they do not directly confront authority and power in recognizable ways. A situated, ethnographic analysis also opens up the possibility of seeing and understanding democratic inclusion and participation in spaces that are assumed to be undemocratic and oppressive.

CONCLUSION

An analysis of interview and participant observation data reveals several consistent findings in relation to gender equality and religious community.

First, some Sikh women uphold and resist exclusionary inclusion from within their religious community. Second, some Sikh women experience religious community as a surprising resource from which to create more egalitarian gender relations. Third, some Sikh women link the goals of gender equality and religious group autonomy; they link the goals of gender-based liberation and spiritual liberation. These findings underscore why it is important to challenge assumptions that characterize religiosity as antithetical to citizenship and religious relations as nondemocratic. This is an open empirical question, which requires empirical research. A situated approach to citizenship forces a rethinking of key categories of analysis, which enables us to see and understand acts of devotion as acts of citizenship, to see and understand democratic participation in the very space assumed to be undemocratic, and to see and understand interconnected understandings of human and divine agency.

The unevenness of religious communities can provide women with a limited opening from which to expand prescribed gender roles and to resist exclusionary inclusion from within religious spaces. This unevenness can enable women to survive and perhaps even thrive in the face of exclusionary inclusion. For some women, a religious community is an unexpected space from which to pursue both spiritual and political liberation, albeit in complicated and contradictory ways.

Conclusion

Reconsidering Politics in Unusual Places

In 2005, I spent the summer in Punjab as part of my ongoing ethnographic research on the intersections between gender, caste, class, religion, and nation, and the implications of these intersections for women's lives and their experience of citizenship. During this time, Biji—my paternal grandmother, who was in Punjab—suffered a stroke, was admitted to the hospital, and eventually passed away. What began as an intellectual endeavor quickly transformed into a deeply personal experience.

My grandmother's funeral began with a ritual bathing and dressing, followed by a procession from our familial home to the local cremation ground. At the public cremation ground, we said our final goodbyes to Biji while listening to Sikh scripture, and then Biji was moved to the funeral pyre. Without much thought, I followed Biji. Within minutes of reaching the funeral pyre, Gupta uncle, a family friend, kindly said in English, "It isn't appropriate for you to be here." As I looked around, I realized that I was the only woman among a large crowd of men. In response, I said in English, "I would like to stay with Biji." He repeated his request again, and I refused again.

As I tried to move closer to Biji, I was forcibly restrained. An older woman grabbed me and pulled me from the location of the funeral pyre. She repeatedly stated in Punjabi, "You will cause harm by being here. Your presence is inauspicious. You will cause harm by being here." As she dragged me away from Biji, I stated in Punjabi, "The harm has already occurred: Biji is dead." I struggled and repeatedly called for my father's help when an unknown man stepped forward, freed me from the older woman's grasp, and permitted me to participate.

I was utterly shocked. How could I cause harm? Whom would I cause harm to? Why did my gender mark me as the source of potential harm and inauspiciousness? And why did my gender mark me as vulnerable to physical violence? Initially, my only response was to think of Biji. When Biji was alive, she referred to me as her beloved child. However, after she passed, at the public cremation ground, I was perceived as her grand-daughter, a gendered identity.

Religious studies scholar Nikky Guninder Kaur Singh (2000, 64–65) notes that at her mother's funeral, she was not allowed to light the funeral pyre:

> Since time immemorial, Indian society has depended on the eldest son to ignite the pyre of his mother and father. . . . In my family, there was only one son. My brother was in the United States. He could not make it to our mother's funeral. Who could be entrusted to per-form his profound duty? A surrogate had to be found. From among all the men surrounding Mother's body, my father asked his former secretary, who had been like a son to my parents, to light the pyre. I did not even question his choice. In the male-defined and male-controlled web of action, I was not even aware of being eliminated.

Just as Singh experienced sexism at her mother's funeral, I experienced it at my grandmother's funeral. My gender limited my mobility, marking me as "other" within the Sikh cremation rites; my gender determined, largely, my vulnerability to physical violence, as well as my inclusion in a public space.

I put my experience in direct relation with the gang rape case and with the findings from the Sikh community to call attention to the dangers that lurk in every case of SGBV, from its most extraordinary and hor-rific expression to the more commonplace and mundane expression in daily life. I have no intention of flattening the extreme difference between these iterations of SGBV. Rather, I highlight the similar logics at play along the entirety of the spectrum. Situating citizenship opens a line of *site*; revealing the shaky ground that subtends all acts of SGBV. Situating citizenship raises the political stakes of understanding citizenship in the ways it is negotiated and reappropriated at the most local of levels. By linking the extremes in such a way, situated citizenship calls us to be alert to the minutest of tremors in our daily life so as to be able to better respond when those tremors move uncontrollably along the fault line of democracy and transform into life- and world-destroying quakes.

LEARNING FROM SITUATED CITIZENSHIP

This book weaves an analysis of the 2012 gang rape with ethnographic data with members of the Sikh community to explore the contradictory nature of Indian democracy. The book asks, why do we find pervasive gender-based discrimination, exclusion, and violence in India when the constitution builds an inclusive democracy committed to gender and caste equality? Through a situated analysis of citizenship, I highlight how citizens understand and experience the promises of formal equality and how they uphold and resist exclusionary inclusion in all spheres of life, from private belief to the institutions of government.

How might a situated approach to citizenship make sense of Jyoti Singh's experience? How might a situated analysis of citizenship explain my experience of exclusion at a public cremation ground? How might situated citizenship make visible the gaps between an abstract promise of equal citizenship and Indian women's complicated and contradictory lived experience of citizenship? How might an examination of Indian women's material and embodied situatedness force a rethinking of taken-for-granted concepts in political science? How might such an approach reveal the ways in which the very definitions of democratic and civic life are resisted and expanded by citizens in unexpected spaces and in unpredictable ways?

Situated citizenship as a theoretical and methodological approach opens up the possibility of *seeing* and *understanding* the gang rape victim's experience as horrifically painful and potentially radical. The horror is clear in what the victim experienced at the hands of fellow citizens and the pain her family, friends, and loved ones felt and continue to feel. What is radical is the insistence that the victim be seen as an equal, rights-bearing citizen who deserves state protection and equal protection vis-à-vis fellow citizens. What is also radical is the insistence that we shift our focus from women's formal, legal inclusion to understanding the gendered nature of this inclusion, thus combating women's exclusionary inclusion in democratic India and beyond.

A situated analysis of citizenship also opens up the possibility for *seeing* and *understanding* varied forms of democratic action that are often overlooked or dismissed by traditional approaches. What is transformative is the insistence that we acknowledge a wide range of actions as political, including the actions of non-Western, nonsecular women, some of whom engage in democratic practice in seemingly undemocratic spaces like religious communities. What is radical is the insistence that we recognize that some secular mechanisms designed for inclusion can exclude, while some forms of devotion that link gender equality and religious freedom as shared goals can include.

A situated approach to citizenship also opens up the possibility of *cogenerating* and *interpreting* new kinds of empirical data that often remains outside the purview of political science. "Imagine datasets that count the continuum of violence such as intimate-partner violence prevalence in conflict-affected settings rather than just 'battle deaths'" (True 2015, 564). Envision scholarship that examines gendered, raced, and epistemic violence perpetrated on the researcher in the research process (Behl 2017a, 2019). Consider scholarship that incorporates the violence that researchers perpetrate on the researched (Dauphinee 2010). By insisting that we weigh "made-in-the-academy concepts" (Pachirat 2012) with embodied lived experience, a situated approach to citizenship reveals the hidden stories of gendered violence and can make actionable the invisible stories of gender-blindness.

A situated approach to citizenship also opens up the possibility of *cogenerating* situated meanings of key concepts and categories that can *create* new forms of "situated knowledge" (Rudolph 2005). Such an approach does not assume an a priori definition of key concepts and then impose this definition on local research settings. Rather, such an approach enables researchers to create concepts from local knowledge in collaboration with research participants.[1] For example, a situated approach to citizenship does not assume a uniform category of woman as a starting point, but rather examines when and how women overcome multiple differences—race, ethnicity, religion, caste, class, nation, and sexuality—to organize and mobilize around shared meanings, interests, and solidarities. This approach is transformative because it is informed by the lived experience of marginalized individuals who fall outside the discipline's rehearsed categories, and therefore it leads to concepts that are open to the fullness and complexity of lived experience and power dynamics. This approach is radical because it makes visible the profoundness of our paradoxical realities by requiring us to keep the tension between logical expectations and lived experience at the center of the analysis.

Lastly, a situated study of citizenship opens up the possibility of *seeing* and *understanding* how power operates within epistemic communities. By situating the researcher in the research process, one becomes aware of miscommunication across epistemic community that, at times, is caused by misunderstanding and, at other times, by outright hostility. As a graduate student, I was often told: "What you are doing isn't political science; you won't finish the PhD; you won't get an academic job."[2] I was often asked about the relationship between my independent and dependent variables, about the measurement and operationalization of my variables, to identify my testable hypotheses, and so on.[3] I struggled to provide coherent answers because I didn't understand then what I understand now: I was being judged by an evaluative criterion that did not match my epistemological and methodological approaches, an evaluative criterion that was seemingly being imposed on the entire field of political science. I was being forced to pick generalizability over contextuality; predictive explanation over contextual understanding; reliability and replicability over transparency and reflexivity (Schwartz-Shea and Yanow 2012). A situated approach to citizenship is transformative because it enables scholars to navigate and negotiate exclusionary inclusion within epistemic communities; it enables researchers to choose other ways of producing knowledge that can open up new theoretical and empirical horizons; it gives researchers concrete tools to uncover a deeper understanding of citizenship's history and future.

In the following section, I discuss the implications of my analysis for the study of democracy, citizenship, and gender equality in India and beyond. Next, I critically reflect on my positionality as diasporic researcher, with attention to the ways participants and I coconstruct the data, and to the ways my own blind spots impact the research process. Lastly, I ask if political science as a discipline is open to new paths of knowledge production.

UNDERSTANDING AND CHALLENGING EXCLUSIONARY INCLUSION IN INDIA AND BEYOND

As a theory and methodology, situated citizenship has explanatory value for understanding exclusionary inclusion in India and beyond. An analysis of situated citizenship can make visible the particular mechanisms of exclusionary inclusion that naturalize gendered and racialized citizenship in other geopolitical locations across the world. Such an analysis can also explain why legal and legislative approaches to inequality and violence are insufficient. In short, situated citizenship—as a theoretical and methodological approach—can make sense of intractable problems, such as why gendered and racialized discrimination, exclusion, and violence exist in communities, countries, and geopolitical systems that have adopted constitutions, laws, and public policies that are inclusive and egalitarian.

What does an ethnographic analysis of Sikh women teach us about the experience of exclusionary inclusion in India? This analysis teaches us that there is no space—state, civic, religious, or private—that guarantees democratic life; there is no space that is experienced as completely liberatory.

Rather, these spaces are experienced as both exclusionary and inclusionary. The uneven nature of these spaces provides women with an opening to expand *and* uphold existing gender roles, and to resist *and* maintain exclusionary inclusion.

This analysis also teaches us that the relationship between state, religious community, and gender is an open empirical question, not one that can be assumed as given. We cannot assume that religious and communal ties are always antithetical to citizenship because they can, at times, provide the resources needed for women to enact citizenship—especially when state and law do not fully guarantee women's rights. We cannot assume that religious communities are wholly oppressive because they can, at times, create openings for more inclusive forms of belonging and membership. Also, we cannot assume a simplistic understanding of agency because, at times, human and divine agency are understood and experienced as interconnected.

As scholars, we must take women's identities and solidarities within religious communities and religious relations as the subject of inquiry. What is required are more situated, contextualized interpretive studies to understand how women from marginalized communities—religious minority, Dalit, tribal, and backward caste—mobilize, organize, and forge solidarities in the face of exclusionary inclusion in ways that both resist and maintain gender-based inequality and violence.

What does a situated analysis of Sikh women's citizenship teach us about the experience of exclusionary inclusion beyond India? This analysis provides a model of how to study lived experiences of unequal democracy across a variety of subordinated demographics. This analysis also serves as a model to explain seemingly insolvable problems in liberal democracies, from the tension between law on the books and law in practice to the inconsistency between an individual's commitment to equality and their racist, sexist, and homophobic behavior.

Why is it so difficult to eradicate inequality and oppression through legal reform? Why is law alone *not* a viable way to secure equality for subordinated groups? When it comes to SGBV, some scholars ask, "Why then, in spite of creating and passing protective laws, does El Salvador [Guatemala,

Honduras, Brazil, etc.] fail to adequately protect women and respond to violence against them" (Walsh and Menjivar 2016a, 2; see also Menjivar 2011; Walsh and Menjivar 2016b; Hume and Wilding 2019). Others ask why Morocco's 2004 family law—Moudawana—that grants unparalleled rights to women is unevenly enforced (Eisenberg 2011). While other scholars ask why racial and gender inequality persist in South Africa when its constitution is lauded as the best in the world and characterized as a human rights landmark (Hassim 2018, 357; Modiri 2018, 295). Still others ask why some forms of rights-based inclusion result in "murderous inclusion—erasure, violence, and abandonment"—of queer citizens in different locations (Haritaworn, Kuntsman, and Posocco 2013, 445–446). These questions demonstrate the significance and relevance of a situated approach to citizenship in an ongoing examination of exclusionary inclusion based on multiple axes of difference, in multiple realms across the globe. For example, one can situate the citizenship of racialized groups, such as African Americans and Latinos, in the United States to understand their uneven experiences of American democracy. Similarly, one can situate the lived experience of minority Muslim communities in multiple locations, including India and the United States, to better understand contradictory democratic experiences. Likewise, one can use situated citizenship to understand the religious and political behavior of devout women across the globe, from conservative Christian women in the United States to devout Muslim women in India.

DIASPORIC RESEARCHER: AN AUTOETHNOGRAPHIC
ANALYSIS OF KNOWLEDGE PRODUCTION

Reflexivity requires researchers to critically reflect on their role in every aspect of the research process.[4] To this end, I ask a series of questions about my role in the field and beyond: How do research participants' perception of me in the field affect what I see or do not see, what I learn or do not learn (Behl 2017a)? How do my commitments as a feminist scholar affect what I see and what I learn? Why do I create the knowledge that

I do, and in whose interest do I create this knowledge (Nagar and Geiger 2007, 271)?

Several aspects of my identity were/are salient. I am a young Punjabi-Sikh woman born in the United States to upper-caste, immigrant parents from Punjab. I am fluent in both English and Punjabi. I practice the Sikh faith, but have not been baptized and do not keep unshorn hair. I am an attractive woman, who is short in stature, petite in build, has dark black hair, and wheat-colored complexion—a complexion that is understood as fair and desirable in India, and nonwhite and undesirable in the United States. When I conducted my fieldwork, I was not married. Even as a graduate student, I was in a significantly higher class than most research participants.

Research participants often saw me as a young diasporic Punjabi-Sikh woman. At other times, research participants saw me as a nonresident Indian or a person of Indian origin. My positionality as a diasporic researcher undoubtedly shaped the interview data. My prior knowledge, Punjabi language mastery, race/ethnicity, religion, and familial contacts enabled me to gain access in a way not available to other researchers. As a perceived insider, participants saw me as more trustworthy, and perhaps this led to more valid data on sensitive topics.

However, I simultaneously encountered disadvantages as a perceived insider. Through my field encounters, I found that research participants enjoyed power over me. I was not seen as an authoritative, legitimate knowledge possessor/producer.[5] As a perceived insider, some research participants held me more accountable for norms of personal behavior. Others found me to be lacking in my adherence to a Sikh way of life. Still others saw me as a girl, not a woman, and as a layperson, not a scholar. Research participants, over whom I theoretically enjoyed power, disavowed my position as knowledge producer through some of the very gendered norms that normalize women's exclusionary inclusion in India—women's religiosity, women's rights and duties, and diaspora.[6]

Through the writing process, I found that as an academic I enjoy "a narrative privilege that others do not" (Dauphinee 2010, 807). And therefore, I must ask, how do I "story" the lives of research participants (Dauphinee

2010, 87)? How do I respond to the "blindness of [my] own blind spots" (Ackerly 2013, 100)? Do my personal politics undermine my ability to comprehend other "lifeworlds" (Mahmood 2005, 197–198)? How do my "emotions" affect my analysis (Chong 2008, 384)? In short, what are my blind spots and how do they impact the research process—cogeneration of data in the field, interpretation of ethnographic data, and dissemination of the research in political science?

One way to respond to these particular questions is through self-reflexivity, which requires researchers to critically reflect on their personal, professional, and structural position within the research process (Harding 1986; Twine and Warren 2000; Brown et. al. 2003; Hawkesworth 2006a, 2006b; Tickner 2006; Nagar and Geiger 2007; Bonilla-Silva and Zuberi 2008; Schwartz-Shea and Yanow 2012; Ackerly and True 2010, 2013). In addition to examining one's personal, professional, and structural positions, scholars also need to be self-reflexive about their emotional positioning (Anzaldúa 2003; Doty 2004; Sangtin Writers and Nagar 2006; Chong 2008; Dauphinee 2010; Isoke 2018).

What is required is that researchers also acknowledge, analyze, and reflect on their emotional reactions to the research process. This "emotional knowledge" (Chong 2008) with respect to research participants, research communities, and academia is part of the cogenerated data and requires analysis. This emotional knowledge is a legitimate and valid source of knowledge generation that should have equal standing (Schwartz-Shea and Yanow 2012, 101 and 151). I use autoethnography to critically reflect on my embodied experience of knowledge making, including emotional knowledge. By doing so, I allow readers to determine the trustworthiness of my claims to knowledge (Behl 2017a).

Through autoethnographic writing, I push back against a cold and detached academic writing style that often obscures the pain, trauma, and injustice of gendered violence (Doty 2004; Dauphinee 2010). I write because gendered violence, for me, is not an abstract concept; it is a lived, embodied experience. I too am a victim. I write because I believe that women's lives should be free of fear of violence. I write because academic accounts of gendered violence fail to tell the full story and fail to reveal the full scope and pain of violence. I recount, for myself and for the reader, the details of Jyoti Singh's horrific assault and murder because it keeps this analysis normatively grounded; because it reminds the writer and reader that lives are at stake; because it highlights the profound tragedy of para-doxical democracy.

CONCLUSION

I end this discussion with a significant question that remains unan-swered: given that political scientists have largely ignored decades of feminist and critical research, is political science as a discipline willing to listen to new forms of knowledge production based on situated studies of citizenship, especially when this knowledge is characterized as invalid?[7] Much is at stake in our capacity to be open to new ways of thinking. I fear that if we are not open to new forms of knowledge, then political scientists will fail to explain a political world in which some citizens are vulnerable to SGBV. I fear that if we are not open to new forms of knowledge, then as a discipline political science will continue to replicate gender-blindness, which will impede our understanding of gendered violence and limit our capacity to achieve gender equality in democratic societies. I fear that if we are not open to interpretive, critical, and feminist approaches, then po-litical science will fail to ask important research questions, will fail to find new sources of empirical data that can lead to theoretical innovation, and will fail to understand why the promise of democratic equality remains unrealized.

CHAPTER 1

1. Under Indian law, the press could not release Jyoti Singh's name. As a result, the press and protestors used several names to refer to Jyoti, including *Nirbhaya* (the fearless one), *Amanat* (treasure), *Damini* (lightning), and *Jagruti* (awareness). Jyoti Singh was a Hindu woman from a backward caste background. See chapter 3.

2. The bus in question was a private bus. Delhi has a mix of public and private buses serving more than seven million people every day. According to the police, the assailants tricked the victim and her friend into believing that the bus was part of the city's public fleet. One of the perpetrators posed as a conductor, called out for passengers, and charged the victim and her friend bus fare (Mandhana and Trivedi 2012).

3. For a detailed discussion of the six perpetrators of the gang rape in Delhi, see Sharma, Agarwal, and Malhotra (2013).

4. Chatterji, Buluswar, and Kaur (2015, 22) categorize India as a "conflicted democracy" where "unceasing everyday and spectacular violence," including sexual violence, coexist with the most enlightened laws on paper.

5. Political science also valorizes objectivity and neutrality, which often enables the discipline to ignore gender and race. For a detailed discussion, see Behl (2017a).

6. Other authors make similar arguments about women's limited citizenship rights. Martha Nussbaum (2001, 4) argues, "Women, in short, lack essential support for leading lives that are fully human. . . . Thus, even when they live in a constitutional democracy such as India, where they are equals in theory, they are second-class citizens in reality." According to Rajeswari Sunder Rajan (2000, 71), "To speak of [Indian] women as rights-bearing individuals . . . is to invoke a situation that does not exist in any meaningful way." Similarly, Angana Chatterji (1990, 46) argues, "The Constitution which is expected to be the ultimate guarantor of democracy confers as inalienable the right to equality on both sexes. However, for women in India this provision to be an equal human being is constitutionally sanctioned and ideally spoken about, but in reality missing. After decades of democracy, despite the minority-sustained women's movements, Indian women are still unequal members of the human community."

7. For a similar critique, see Sunder Rajan (2003, 147–176); Ganguly (2003).

8. For a similar critique, see Rai (1996, 11–13); Menon (1999, 275–283); Menon (2004, 3–9); Singh (2015, 661–663).

9. Likewise, Rajeswari Sunder Rajan (2003, 153) argues, "Religion in modern India is not simply a survival of premodern belief systems and religious authority . . . but a crucial signifier of community identity and hence a player in state politics."

10. Shirin Rai (1994, 225) makes a similar argument: "To universalize the experience of western liberal democracies can only lead to intellectual and political cul-de-sacs in the Third World."

11. In the Indian context, caste is a hereditary system of stratification based on intergroup marriage. One's caste, or jati, is associated with one's occupation, and often determines one's material, social, and political power. In Sikhism, no scriptural sanction exists for caste distinction, yet a caste hierarchy still exists (McLeod 1975; Dhami 1995; Mann 2001; Puri 2003). Some Muslims and Christians also adhere to the caste system even though caste is not recognized in Islam or Christianity.

12. According to the Indian Census (2011a), approximately 80 percent of Indians are Hindu, 13 percent are Muslims, 2 percent are Christian, and 2 percent are Sikhs. Approximately 2 percent identify with Buddhism, Jainism, animism, Zoroastrianism, or Judaism.

13. Members of tribal groups—called Adivasis—constitute approximately 8 percent of the population. These groups are recognized in the constitution as eligible for affirmative action measures.

14. Citizenship is often understood as formal, legal status determined by the constitution, which in the Indian case guarantees gender and caste equality. The constitution, adopted by the Indian Constituent Assembly in November 1949, creates a radically more egalitarian model of democracy, what Jawaharlal Nehru referred to as the "fullest democracy," which abolishes discrimination based on religion, race, caste, and sex. Similarly, religious membership and belonging is often determined by religious laws and prescriptions, which in the Sikh case also guarantees gender and caste equality. The Sikh ethical code, Rahit Maryada, adopted by the Shiromani Gurdwara Prabandhak Committee (SGPC) in 1931, creates a radically more egalitarian model of religious practice, which also abolishes discrimination on the basis of religion, caste, race, class, and gender.

15. Agana Chatterji, Shashi Buluswar, and Mallika Kaur (2015, 45) argue that gender violence includes "sexual, as well as economic and psychological violence." Similarly, Sally Engle Merry (2009, 4) argues that "gender violence is both physical and sexual . . . gender violence includes threats, harassment, and stalking—actions that evoke fear even when there is no physical harm. . . . A lack of care such as withholding money or food . . . can also be considered violence."

16. Sally Engle Merry (2009, 2) finds that "violence in intimate relationships is inseparable from societal conflict, violence, and injustice." Similarly, Agana Chatterji, Shashi Buluswar, and Mallika Kaur (2015, 49) find that "conflict-related gendered and sexualized violence is dependent on the equitability of relations between genders in ordinary times." Likewise, Jacqui True (2015, 555–556) argues "private sphere domestic violence [is] both a form of political violence . . . and a precondition for more visible violence against women in the public sphere."

17. For a detailed discussion of the differences between violence against women, gender violence, and violent reproduction of gender, see Shepherd (2007).

18. According to Agana Chatterji, Shashi Buluswar, and Mallika Kaur (2015, 45), "Gendered violence targets all non-dominantly gendered subjects regardless of their gender status (as cisgender or transgender, multigender) or sexuality (as LGBTIQA)." According to Sally Engle Merry (2009, 1), both women and men are the victims of gender violence, but women experience this violence at disproportionately higher rates. Merry (2009, 1) finds that "male rape in prison, torture of men in wartime, patterns of hazing and harassment in male organizations, and homophobic assaults on gay men are only a few of the kinds of violence directed against men."

19. Similarly, Banerjee et al. (2004, 132–133) argue that the "study of gendered violence . . . should operate not just as shorthand for understanding violence on and against women, but also as an analytical category that is equally attentive to the ways in which normative ideas of masculinity and heterosexuality are disseminated."

20. According to Angana Chatterji (1990, 47), "[Indian] women as a community are too subjugated and oppressed to demand equality or benefits as a right. They are vulnerable because they are powerless. To be equal human beings their rights need not only to be legalized but should also receive social acceptance. This requires attitudinal changes."

CHAPTER 2

1. According to a perception poll conducted by TrustLaw, India is the worst place to be a woman among G20 nations, while Canada is the best (Baldwin 2012; Bhalla 2012). Similarly, the Thomson Reuters Foundation's 2018 Survey of the World's Most Dangerous Countries for Women named India as the most dangerous country for women based on three criteria—the risk for sexual violence and harassment, danger from cultural, tribal, and traditional practices, and risk for human trafficking.

2. Objective measures characterize India as a free, fully institutionalized democracy. Polity IV characterizes India as democratic, with a score in +6 to +9 range (−10 being most autocratic and +10 being most democratic). Freedom House characterizes India as free with a political rights score of 2 and a civil liberties score of 3 (1 being the most free and 7 the least free).

3. India, unlike most of the Western developed world, guaranteed women's enfranchisement prior to the ratification of the Indian constitution. In the following countries, women's enfranchisement was won through long and sustained feminist struggles: the United States, the United Kingdom, New Zealand, France, Canada, Belgium, Australia, Germany, Italy, and Switzerland.

4. For further detail, see Kapur and Cossman (1999); Nussbaum (2001, 2002); Trivedi (2003); Kapur (2007); Keating (2007); Roy (2014).

5. For a detailed discussion of how personal law effectively suspends women's most basic rights on behalf of group rights, see chapter 3.

6. It is difficult to obtain reliable statistics for violence against women in India, because rape within marriage is not counted as a crime, penile penetration was a

necessary element of rape in Indian law until recently, and women are deterred from reporting crimes. For a detailed discussion, see chapter 3.

7. In comparison, 55 percent of women in Kigali, Rwanda, and 25 percent of women in Paris, France, feel unsafe in public spaces (United Nations Women, 2012 Survey).

8. The survey also found that respondents perceive sexual harassment as the biggest risk for women's safety and identify roads (50 percent), public transportation (39 percent), and markets (22 percent) as most unsafe public spaces (United Nations Women, 2012 Survey).

9. According to the United Nations Office on Drugs and Crime (2010), the rape rate in India is 1.7. The mean rape rate is 11.7 and the median rape rate is 5.2. The five highest rape rates: South Africa (113.5), Australia (91.6), Swaziland (76.1), Canada (68.2), and Jamaica (50.8). The five lowest rape rates: Pakistan (0), Egypt (0.2), Armenia (0.3), Maldives (0.3), and Azerbaijan (0.4). The lower rape rates in India can be attributed to underreporting, lack of reliable data, and differences in the definition of rape. The UN rape rate is calculated per 100,000 population (United Nation Office on Drugs and Crime 2010). According to R. Amy Elman (2013, 240), differing conceptions of crime, including rape, and varying methods of record keeping complicate rigorous comparative scholarship on gendered violence. Elman (2013, 240) argues "a dearth of reported incidents could also suggest limited faith in the state's capacity to rectify sexist oppression." Conversely, Elman finds that "a higher level of reporting may indicate both a greater awareness among women and girls that their abuse is criminal and a confidence in the state to respond accordingly" (240).

10. The Thomson Reuters Foundation's 2017 World's Most Dangerous Cities for Women survey found Delhi to be the fourth most dangerous city in the world for women. When it comes to sexual violence and harassment, the survey ranked Delhi and São Paulo as the world's most dangerous cities for women.

11. Most rape victims find it very difficult to register police complaints. Often a rape victim's sexual history is used against her, medical evidence is not taken promptly, police delay in processing complaints, and sometimes police sexually assault women who report crimes.

12. According to the United Nations Women 2012 Delhi survey, when respondents were asked what factors put women at risk for violence in public spaces, the number one response was gender. Gender, more so than age, religion, disability, and state/region, puts women at risk (United Nations Women, 2012 Delhi Survey). According to Shirin Rai (1994, 217), "It is not just the act of rape but the threat of rape that keeps women inside the home, out of the public sphere."

13. A similar argument can be made for race. Teri Caraway (2004, 457) argues, "By confining the study of democratization to the incorporation of [white] men, the picture of the politics of democratization is skewed." In response, Caraway (2004, 457) calls for an integration of gender and race into analyses of democratization because using gender and race as analytic categories will transform the field into "more than just studies of the enfranchisement of white men . . . [and] make clear the gender and racial assumptions that underlie much of comparative political analysis."

14. According to Caroline Beer (2009, 212), "Many prominent democracy scholars find no contradiction in categorizing political systems as 'democratic' even when the female half of the population was prohibited from participating in government." Similarly, Georgina Waylen (2007, 15) finds that "the mainstream democratization literature has remained largely gender-blind, with very little to say about the participation of women in transitions to democracy or the gendered nature of those processes."

15. For a detailed discussion of democratization scholarship and women's role in transitions to democracy, see Rai (1994); Waylen (2007). For a detailed discussion of democratization scholarship and gendered citizenship, see Behl (2014).

16. Paxton (2000, 103) finds that measures of democracy that include women challenge the widely held belief that Western democracies are older and more inclusive than less-developed nations.

17. According to Waylen (2007, 16) there are three dominant definitions of democracy. "At one end of the continuum, a narrow Schumpterian approach uses a minimal . . . one-dimensional procedural definition, [under which] a large number of systems are democracies." Next is Dahl's polyarchy: a two-dimensional definition focused on universal adult franchise and electoral contestation, which characterizes fewer countries as democratic. Last is a more robust, multidimensional definition of democracy, requiring that citizens enjoy civil, political, and social rights, which characterizes most countries as undemocratic. As Waylen notes, based on a procedural definition of democracy, women's suffrage is not required to be categorized as democratic. Based on a two-dimension definition, women's civil and political rights are required. Only multidimensional definitions of democracy consider women's civil, political, and social rights as necessary for democracy (Waylen 2007, 16).

18. Pamela Paxton (2000, 92) finds that leading democratization scholars "commonly use male suffrage as the sole indicator of a country's transition to democracy." This leads to the absurd situation in which definitions of democracy include universal adult suffrage, yet measures of democracy include only male suffrage. In short, "measures of democracy do not match theoretical definitions" (Paxton 2000, 92). For example, Caroline Beer (2009, 221) finds that most democratization scholarship relies on Polity IV dataset, defined as executive recruitment, independence of executive authority, and political competition, which "does not incorporate women's suffrage." As a result, Switzerland, for example, "received a perfect Polity IV score of 10 on democracy even when women were not permitted to vote" (Beer 2009, 221).

19. Critical legal studies and critical race studies are distinct intellectual projects with shared radical left beginnings. According to Kimberlé Crenshaw (1995, xxvi–xxvii), "We [critical race theorists] see CLS [critical legal studies] and CRT [critical race theory] as aligned—in radical left opposition to mainstream legal discourse. But CRT is also different from CLS—our focus on race means that we have addressed quite different concerns, with distinct methodologies and traditions that we honor." Cornel West (1995, xi) makes this distinction in a more forceful way: "They [CRT scholars] not only challenged basic assumptions and presuppositions of the

prevailing paradigms among mainstream liberals and conservatives in the legal academy, but also confronted the relative silence of legal radicals—namely critical legal studies writers—who 'deconstructed' liberalism, yet seldom addressed the role of deep-seated racism in American life."

20. Patricia Williams (1991, 11) finds that "the myth of the purely objective perspective . . . [is] too often reified in law as 'impersonal' rules and 'neutral' principles, presumed to be inanimate, unemotional, unbiased, unmanipulated, and higher than ourselves." Likewise, Cornel West (1988, 756–757) argues that such assumptions and presuppositions "hide and conceal systemic relations of power that continue to encourage bloodshed and inhibit people's well-being." Similarly, Kimberlé Crenshaw (1995, xxv) argues that "the legal system is thoroughly involved in constructing the rules of the game, in selecting the eligible players, and in choosing the field on which the game must be played."

21. West (1988, 766) argues that "partiality and partisanship are at work in the dispassionate styles and forms of liberal discourse [that justify] operations of power that scar human bodies, delimit life-chances for many, and sustain privilege for some." Similarly, Mari Matsuda ([1988] 1992, 299) finds that "abstraction . . . is the method that allows theorists to discuss liberty, property, and rights in the aspirational mode of liberalism with no connection to what those concepts mean in real people's lives."

22. Menon (2004, 4) argues that law is limited in its emancipatory potential because "(a) Most legal systems have features which are actively discriminatory . . . (b) Even where there is *de jure* equality, law in its actual functioning discriminates . . . (c) It is unjust to treat unequals equally . . . (d) The law and the state render invisible women's subjective experience of oppression since objectivity is installed as the norm."

23. Chantal Mouffe (1992, 4) calls on us "to go beyond the conceptions of citizenship of both the liberal and the civic republican traditions while building on their respective strengths." Similarly, Ruth Lister (1997a, 28) calls for a "synthesis of rights and participatory approaches to citizenship . . . as the basis for a feminist theory of citizenship."

24. According to David Held, "Citizenship has meant a reciprocity of rights against, and duties towards, the community. Citizenship has entailed membership, membership of the community in which one lives one's life. And membership has invariably involved degrees of participation in the community" (1991, 20).

25. According to Michael Walzer (1989, 216), "We have, then, two different understandings of what it means to be a citizen. The first describes [republican] citizenship as an office, a responsibility, a burden proudly assumed; the second describes [liberal] citizenship as a status, an entitlement, a right or set of rights passively enjoyed. The first makes citizenship the core of our life, the second makes it its outer frame. The first assumes a closely knit body of citizens, its members committed to one another; the second assumes a diverse and loosely connected body, its members (mostly) committed elsewhere. According to the first, the citizen is the primary political actor, law-making and administration his everyday business.

According to the second, law-making and administration are someone else's business; the citizen's business is private."

26. Republican conceptions of citizenship move beyond the liberal model in which "individual citizens are reduced to atomized, passive bearers of rights whose freedom consists in being able to pursue their individual interests" (Lister 1997a, 32).

27. According to Bryan Turner (1990, 190), "This renewed interest in the issue of social participation and citizenship rights has, in turn, resulted, at the theoretical level, in a revival of interest in the work of T. H. Marshall . . . which provides an important point of departure for any debate about the contemporary complexities of the relationship between citizenship entitlements and the economic structure of capitalist society."

28. According to Yuval-Davis (1997, 6), "Studying citizenship can throw light on . . . the complex relationships between individuals, collectivities and the state." Similarly, Lister (1997a, 29) argues, citizenship is "not simply a set of legal rules governing the relationship between individuals and the state . . . but also a set of social relationships between . . . individual citizens." Lastly, Rocco (2004, 16) argues that "citizenship is not solely . . . a legal status, but rather a political mechanism for the control and containment of access to institutions of power and of the distribution of rights."

29. Weldon (2013, 85) outlines a wide range of activities "including—but by no means limited to—violence against women; religious practices and organization; reproductive rights; language; crime; non-state violence; ethnic conflict; communalism; family structure; national identities; the contested nature of culture and tradition; social citizenship and inclusion; protest and other activities outside the purview of the state."

30. Republican approaches to citizenship are also problematic because of "the demanding nature of republican citizenship which has particular implications for women, disadvantaged by the sexual division of time; its narrow conception of the 'political' . . . ; and its uncritical appeal to notions of universalism, impartiality and the common good" (Lister 1997a, 33).

31. For a detailed discussion of the debates surrounding intersectionality, see Collins and Chepp (2013); Dhamoon (2013); and Hancock (2016). For a discussion of the relevance of intersectionality for political science, see Dhamoon (2011); Hancock and Simien (2011); Hankivsky and Cormier (2011); Townsend-Bell (2011); Wadsworth (2011); Brown (2014); and Sampaio (2015). For a comparative analysis of intersectionality outside the US context, see Bassel and Lepinard (2014); Siim (2014); Lepinard (2014); Bassel and Emejulu (2014); and Townsend-Bell (2014).

32. African American scholar Kimberlé Crenshaw (1989, 1991) developed the term "intersectionality" to explain how some individuals experience racial and gender discrimination simultaneously and in a compound fashion. A number of feminists in the US context and beyond have further developed Crenshaw's original idea (King 1988; Brah and Phoenix 2004; Phoenix and Pattynama 2006; Yuval-Davis 2006a; Puar 2007; Hancock 2007a, 2007b). However, some social science scholars have taken up intersectionality in such a way as to "disappear" black women

(Alexander-Floyd 2012). Others "whiten" intersectionality by erasing its roots in black feminist thought (Bilge 2013a, 2013b). Still others deploy intersectionality as an analytic tool without its original "liberatory" framework (Jordan-Zachery 2007).

33. Susanne Rudolph (2005, 12) defines situated knowledge as "knowledge marked by place, time, and circumstance—[which] relies on the excavation of meaning....Situated knowledge ... is committed to the validity and significance of local knowledge—to the way peoples understand their histories, social processes, and worldviews. . . . Situated knowledge thus makes visible and credible a variety of forms of life."

34. I draw on scholarship by women of color who found themselves in a double bind because they were marginalized as women in in antiracist movements and as racialized minorities in the feminist movement. These scholars argued that they experienced multiple interlocking forms of subordinations, which were overlooked in antiracist and feminist struggles. In response, they called for pluralism within both movements to ensure sensitivity to and inclusion of difference (Combahee River Collective [1977] 1997; hooks 1981, 1994; Anzaldúa and Moraga 1981; Feminist Review 1984; Collins 1986, 1989, 1990; Anzaldúa 1987; King 1988; Crenshaw 1989, 1991; Grewal and Kaplan 1994; Mohanty 2003; Brah and Phoenix 2004; Yuval-Davis 2006a; Barvosa 2008).

35. According to Glenn (2011, 2), "Law and political science usually view citizenship as a formal status defined by legal documents and state policies. Thus, legal and political scholars focus on constitutions, laws, court decisions, and the writings and speeches of influential legal and political actors."

36. I draw from Glenn's (2002, 2011) historical analysis of citizenship in the United States. Glenn (2011, 3) finds that linear and progressive approaches to citizenship cannot account for the "the complexity, dynamism, and fluidity of citizenship in the United States." In response, Glenn (2011, 2) advances an understanding of citizenship as "continually constituted and challenged through political struggle."

37. An expanded notion of politics can be traced to multiple sources: feminist literature (Crowley et al. 1997; Lister 1997a; Yuval-Davis 1997, 2006; Alcoff 2006), New Left scholarship (Hobsbawm 1980; Scott 1985, 1989, 1990), subaltern studies (Guha and Spivak 1988; Guha 1988), and scholarship on race (Kelley 1994; Hanchard 2006). In all of these literatures, "Power is seen as simultaneously pervasive and dispersed in social relations of all kinds, not just those conventionally thought of as political" (Glenn 2002, 16).

38. For a detailed discussion of grounded normative political theory, experience-informed grounded approaches, and feminist grounded normative theory, see Ackerly (2018, 135–153).

39. For a detailed discussion, see Behl (2017b).

40. Historically, ethnography has been deployed as a methodological and epistemological tool to justify, legitimize, and promote colonialism, slavery, racism, orientalism, and more (Isoke 2018; Pachirat 2018). According to Zenzele Isoke (2018, 153), "Ethnography is a loaded term. It is loaded with the heavy cargo of slave ships, military invasion, and cultural annihilation. Ethnography invented the other. It made the other 'dirty,' 'savage,' 'wicked,' 'lascivious,' 'backward,' 'uncouth.' The ethnographer made the other black. A stranger unto herself. The ethnographer

rendered the black body placeless and dispossessed of a history, a culture, a language or a name. The Ethnographer made Man in his own image: murderous, greedy, and parasitic. And made the other as its opposite: life-giving, generous, and vulnerable. The Ethnographer made himself rational, economical, and geographic and made the other erotic, abundant, and metaphysical."

41. Demographic (Henderson 2009; Islam 2000; Ortbals and Rincker 2009; Townsend-Bell 2009) and locational (Pachirat 2009; Zirakzadeh 2009) positionalities can influence access during the research process.

42. For a detailed discussion, see Schatz (2009, 10–12).

43. Snowball sampling is used in two situations: research on hard-to-reach populations and research requiring trust. Snowball sampling is useful because it provides access to previously hidden or stigmatized populations; creates trust between researcher and researched; and provides an economical and effective way of sampling. Snowball sampling is limited because the sample is not a representative, random sample, and therefore one cannot make claims of generalizability; the sampling method requires prior knowledge of insiders to initiate the chain referral; and the method depends on respondents to participate in the chain referral (Atkinson and Flint 2001).

44. For a detailed discussion of ethnographic, in-depth, semi-structured, and relational interviews, see Fujji (2018, 7–9).

45. For example, I asked participants to describe themselves, describe their identity, and explain how others describe them.

46. The first segment is *amritdhari*, those who keep unshorn hair and have undergone the baptismal ceremony. The second is *kesdhari*, those who keep hair but have not been baptized. The third category refers to *sahijdhari,* those who do not keep unshorn hair and have not undergone the baptismal ceremony (Mann 2004, 99).

CHAPTER 3

1. The way these debates get framed—sati in colonial and postcolonial discourse (Mani 1987, 1990; Sangari and Vaid 1999b), violence against women in international discourse (Kapur 2002), or gang rape in postcolonial discourse (Behl 2017b)—has implications for how women's equality is understood.

2. Feminist scholars are divided on the relationship between multiculturalism and feminism. This division is primarily animated by the following question: "How can we reconcile the justified demand of minority groups for recognition of their religious, ethnic, or cultural identity with the feminist goal of the individual autonomy of women?" (Baukje 2006, 234). For some, multiculturalism is understood as antithetical to gender equality because it enables men to control women within the confines of their traditional, patriarchal communities (Okin 1999; Wikan 2002; Hirsi Ali 2006). For others, multiculturalism is not opposed to feminism, but is seen as compatible with it. For a detailed discussion of cultural rights, see Das (1999); Baukje (2006).

3. Sunder Rajan (2003, x) outlines how the Indian state has "sponsored reports, set up commissions, involved women's groups in the drafting of laws . . . and subscribed to international norms of gender equality." For Sunder Rajan (2003, x), this

contradictory and uneven functioning of the state as it relates to women must be "taken into account for both a theory and a praxis of feminism."

4. For a detailed discussion, see Sunder Rajan (2003).

5. Likewise, Shirin Rai and Geraldine Lievesley (1996, 4) find that the state in Third World settings provides "opportunities for both progress and regression in the struggle for women's emancipation."

6. India is a constitutional parliamentary democracy, with written Fundamental Rights containing extensive equality provisions: Article 14 guarantees equality; Article 15 restricts the state from sex-based discrimination; Article 16 guarantees equal opportunity; Article 39.d guarantees equal pay for equal work; and Article 19 guarantees freedom of speech and expression, freedom of association, freedom of travel, freedom of residence, and freedom to form labor unions. For further detail, see Kapur and Cossman (1999); Nussbaum (2001, 2002); Trivedi (2003); and Keating (2007).

7. For a detailed discussion, see Agnes (1996); Sunder Rajan (2000, 2003); Rudolph and Rudolph (2000); Nussbaum (2001, 2002); Williams (2006); Robinson (2010); Htun and Weldon (2011); and Bajpai (2011).

8. For a detailed discussion, see Keating (2007, 2011).

9. Sikh nationalists often trace the roots of nationalism to Guru Gobind Singh, who created the institution of the Khalsa (pure), and vested Sikh authority and sovereignty in the Guru Granth and in the community (Guru Panth) (P. Singh 2014, 24). Creation of the Khalsa as the sovereign authority of the Sikhs is referenced as an early manifestation of a Sikh nation, and is used to provide continuity between the Guru period and colonial and postcolonial struggles for a separate Sikh nation-state, Khalistan. Postcolonial Sikh nationalism draws on religious history, tradition, memories, and myths to create solidarity and continuity for a Sikh nation. Sikh nationalists, including Sant Jarnail Singh Bhindranwale, the leader of the 1980s Sikh secessionist movement, envisioned themselves as fighting for a true Sikh state free from Indian secularism, which functions as "a thin disguise for Hindu religious and cultural imperialism" (Embree 1990, 126).

10. According to Menon (1999b, 16), "The Direct Principles of state policy call for the state to enact a uniform civil code, but successive governments have not so far done so, because the personal laws are protected by the Fundamental Right to freedom of religion."

11. According to Menon (1999b, 31), "The demand for a Uniform Civil Code for all religious communities was first made by the All India Women's Conference in 1937. Sixty years later, this demand is certainly not made by the Indian women's movement with the same confidence. By 1993, at the Northern Region Nari Mukti Sangharsh Sammelan (Women's Liberation Struggle Conference) held in Kanpur, there were two resolutions put forward for debate, one calling for a UCC, and the other for a rethinking of the notion of uniformity. . . . And at the Fifth National Conference of Women's Studies held in Jaipur in 1995, what emerged was a broad range of positons, from the reassertion of the demand for a UCC, to outright rejection of such a move, and calling instead for reforms within personal law."

12. For a detailed discussion, see Sunder Rajan (2000, 2003); Keating (2011).

13. According to Das (2007, 21), "The story about abduction and recovery acts as a foundational story that authorizes a particular relation between social contract and sexual contract—the former being a contract between men to institute the political and the latter the agreement to place women within the home under the authority of the husband/father figure."

14. For a detailed discussion, see Kabeer (2015).

15. For a detailed discussion, see Kale (2013) and Lodhia (2015).

16. According to Sharmila Lodhia (2015, 98), the new law "elevated the interests of the imagined family, 'national security,' and a narrow framework of acceptable intimacies through its refusal to embed the more progressive recommendations of the Verma Committee."

17. For a detailed discussion, see Hodge (2013); Roychowdhury (2013); Lodhia (2015); Kabeer (2015); and Datta (2016). Indian news media also maintain and perpetuate caste- and class-bias when it comes to violence against women by focusing on sexual violence against middle-class and upper-caste women and overlooking violence against poor, rural, lower-class, lower-caste, and marginalized women. For a detailed discussion, see Rao (2014).

18. For a detailed discussion about the victim and her family, see Pokharel et al. (2013).

19. For a detailed discussion, see Baxi (2012); Hodge (2013); and Basu (2013).

20. For a detailed discussion, see Roychowdhury (2013).

21. Women's activist organizations, which have been advocating gender justice for decades, as well as lawyers, law students, and academics contributed extensively to the JVC process. Their knowledge was highly valued and was explicitly acknowledged (2013, ii).

22. For a detailed discussion, see Kale (2013); Lodhia (2015).

23. Similarly, Lodhia (2015, 95) finds that political figures explain gendered violence by blaming the victim: "She invited the attack, she wore the wrong clothes, she went out at night, and she was too Westernized."

24. It is important to note that Mohan Bhagwat is not an elected official and the RSS is not a political party. Rather, the RSS is the voluntary, religious wing of the Bharatiya Janata Party, a right-wing, Hindu nationalist party.

25. Menon (1999a, 286) distinguishes between law reform strategies and litigation strategies: "Law reform strategies seek to bring about new legislation to give legal recognition to rights-claims, while litigation strategies use existing laws either aggressively or defensively to advance such claims. It should be clear that it is the latter strategy which I see as the only possible engagement with the law that will not comprise our ethical vision."

26. Scholars of race and ethnicity also make a similar claim. Rogers Brubaker (2004, 9) argues that ethnicity "is a key part of what we want to explain, not what we want to explain things *with*; it belongs to our empirical data, not to our analytic toolkit." Similarly, Taeku Lee (2008, 461) argues, "An expectation of a preordained identity-to-politics link can potentially distort our understanding of race and ethnicity, especially when taken as prior to, rather than subject to, empirical study." Cristina Beltran (2010, 12) finds that scholars "too often take for granted the very categories and practices they ought to be analyzing and calling into question."

27. The Sikh population has been "historically concentrated in three geographical areas in the Punjab: the Majha, in the north, the Doaba, in the center, and the Malwa, in the south" (Mann 2006, 44). Until the middle of the twentieth century, Sikhs largely married within their areas of birth and within their caste group. However, with growing migration within and outside of Punjab, these geographic differences have diluted. Caste differences, however, continue to be significant.

28. J. S. Grewal (1990, 30) describes Nanak's new vision in the following way: "The *shudra* and the untouchable are placed at par with the Brahman and the Khatri. The woman is placed at par with the man. The differences of caste and sex, and similarly the differences of country and creed, are set aside as irrelevant for salvation."

29. Nikky Guninder Kaur Singh (1993, 46) states: "There are no priests, no commentators, no rituals, no philosophical doctrines, no societal or gender hierarchies that stand in between a person and the sacred poetry. Authority—that of the *pandit* in Hinduism, of the *ulama* in Islam, of the rabbi in Judaism—that would interpret for the person his or her duty, has no place in the direct poetic encounter."

30. Avtar Brah (2005, 159–160) describes Sikh philosophy as "a philosophy that advocates an egalitarian vision, espouses a fundamental dismantling of caste hierarchy, critiques women's subordination, and proposes a spiritual practice that does away with the mediations of the male cleric or the esoteric priestly caste so that anyone, male or female; black, brown, or white could officiate at the performance of rituals; and finally, a philosophy that permits direct access to 'the Formless Infinite' through a very simple practice of meditation on the Name that can be carried out anywhere, rather than being restricted to a place of worship."

31. *Langar* not only encourages individuals to "sit in status-free line (*pangat*) and eat together," but also requires individuals to eat food that has been offered, prepared, and served by others irrespective of religion, caste, gender, and class differences (McLeod 1989, 12–13).

32. The baptismal ceremony, *khande di pahul*, initiated by the tenth guru, Gobind Singh, also undermines caste hierarchies by questioning notions of ritual purity. The ceremony requires all participants to drink *amrit* (nectar, or water used for baptism) from a common bowl without assigning any significance to the caste background of those who administer and partake in the ceremony (Mann 2001, 93). In addition to requiring participants to drink from the same bowl, the *khande di pahul* ceremony further reinforces caste equality because it is believed that the first five to accept baptism "included a representative range from high-caste Khatri through middle-caste Jat to low-caste barber and washerman" (McLeod 1975, 86). The *khande di pahul* ceremony is an embodied practice that undermines the logic of purity and pollution by requiring individual Sikhs of all caste backgrounds to drink *amrit* from a common bowl.

33. The practice of distributing *karah parshad* (blessed food) in *gurdwaras* also undermines notions of ritual purity. The practice is significant not only in the actual presentation of the blessed food, but also in its subsequent consumption. *Karah parshad* can be offered by anyone. These offerings are then deposited into a single dish and a portion is distributed to everyone who is present in the congregation.

The distribution of *karah parshad*, according to McLeod (1975, 86–87), "ensures that high castes consume food received in effect from the hands of lower castes or even outcastes and that they do so from a common dish."

34. Amritdhari Sikhs are required to wear the following five items: *kachha* (shorts), *kes* (hair), *kangha* (comb), *kirpan* (sword), and *kara* (steel bracelet).

35. Ground-level realities also demonstrate that, historically, gender inequality in the Sikh community has varied, in part based on caste affiliation. For example, female infanticide was a problem among Khatri Sikhs, particularly Bedis and Sodhis, during the late nineteenth century. According to W. H. McLeod (1995, 65), "Among Sikhs the practice was particularly prevalent with the Bedis, a result of their high social and ritual status. It was essential to marry daughters to a higher subcaste (got), but because they occupied the highest rank of their section of the zat the Bedis had nowhere to go. Often they preferred infanticide as the solution . . . midwives were instructed to sometimes kill a newborn if it was female by turning the baby's face into the placenta so that she suffocated in her mother's blood. Other methods were strangulation, feeding drops of akk da dudh (calotropis procera) mixed with gur (raw sugar), or burying alive" (McLeod 1995, 65).

36. For detailed discussion, see McLeod (1975); Dhami (1995); Mann (2001); and Puri (2003).

37. According to Harish Puri, Jats, who were the ruling class under Maharaja Ranjit Singh, remain on top of the hierarchy, followed by Khatris and Aroras, and Dalits at the bottom. However, he also states that "the perceptions regarding which caste is placed second, third and fourth varied both by the village and the caste one belonged to" (2003, 2697–2698). In contrast, Gurinder S. Mann (2001, 94–95) places the urban Khatri and Arora segment of the community, who originally come from upper-caste Hindu background, at the top of the hierarchy, followed by Jats, and then backward and scheduled castes.

38. In addition to Chamars and Chuhras, the Sikh Dalit community has members from the following groups: "Chhimas (tailors), Jhinvar (water carriers), Lohars (blacksmiths), Nais (barbers), and Ramgarias (carpenters)" (Mann 2001, 95).

39. Sikhs secured Dalit recognition following independence. In 1948, one of the major demands put forward by all the twenty-two Sikh members of the East Punjab legislative assembly involved securing for the former untouchable castes converted to Sikhism the same recognition and rights as would have been available to them if they had not become Sikhs. Sikh leadership worried that if reservation benefits were not extended to low-caste Sikhs, then they may leave the Sikh fold (Puri 2003, 2699; Jodhka 2004, 179).

40. In India, the sex ratio measures the number of females per 1,000 males, whereas in the rest of the world the sex ratio measures number of males per 100 females. For comparative purposes, in 2011 the sex ratio by religion was Hindus 931:1000, Christians 1009:1000, Buddhists 953:1000, and Jains 940:1000 (Indian Census 2011a). In 2011, in Punjab the sex ratio was 895:1000 and the child sex ratio was 846:1000. In 2001, the sex ratio in Punjab was 874:1000 and the child sex ratio was 961:1000 (Indian Census 2011c). For comparative purposes, in 2011 the Indian sex ratio was 943:1000 and the child sex ratio was 919:1000. In 2001, the Indian sex

ratio was 933:1000 and the child sex ratio was 927:1000. In 2011, the five states /
union territories with the highest sex ratio were Kerala (1084), Puducherry (1038),
Tamil Nadu (995), Andhra Pradesh (992), and Chhattisgarh (991). In 2011, the five
states with the lowest sex ratio were Daman & Diu (618), Dadra & Nagar Haveli
(775), Chandigarh (818), NCT of Delhi (866), and Andaman & Nicobar Islands
(878). In 2011, the states / union territories with the highest child sex ratio were
Mizoram (971), Meghalaya (970), Andaman & Nicobar Islands (966), Puducherry
(965), and Chhattisgarh (964). In 2011, the states and union territories with the
lowest child sex ratio were Haryana (830), Punjab (846), Jammu & Kashmir (859),
NCT of Delhi (866), and Chandigarh (867) (Indian Census 2011b). Compare
Western industrialized nations' ratios of males and females to India's ratio: India
1.12; the United States 1.05; the United Kingdom 1.05; Denmark 1.06; Finland 1.04;
Switzerland 1.05; and France 1.05 (CIA World Factbook 2012).

41. For a detailed discussion, see Miller (1981); Gupta (1987); Chhachhi (1989); Booth
and Verma (1992); Sen (1992, 2003); Mutharayappa et al. (1997); Jha et al. (2006);
Sahni et al. (2008); Purewal (2010, 2014); United Nations Women (2014).

42. In comparison, 53 percent of Hindu women are literate, compared to 76 percent of
Hindu men; 50 percent of Muslim women are literate, compared to 68 percent of
Muslim men; and 76 percent of Christian women are literate, compared to 84 percent of Christian men. Also, 27 percent of Hindu women participate in the labor
market, compared to 52 percent of Hindu men; 14 percent of Muslim women participate in the labor market, compared to 48 percent of Muslim men; and 29 percent of Christian women participate in the labor market, compared to 51 percent of
Christian men (Indian Census 2011a).

CHAPTER 4

1. Harsimran Kaur Sagoo and Rupinder Kaur are founding members of the Mata
Gujri Sukhmani Seva Society Sukhmani Seva Society (see chapter 5). Kaur, Sagoo,
and I were at the local *gurdwara* seated in front of the Guru Granth as Kaur made
these statements. It is important to note Sagoo's reaction. Sagoo did not interrupt
Kaur, nor did she correct Kaur's mischaracterization of Sikh scripture. However,
through Sagoo's body language it was clear that she was surprised by Kaur's interpretation of Sikh scripture as it relates to women's purity. I did not explore the
tensions between both women's responses, in part, because I did not want to cause
tension in their friendship.

2. Edwina Barvosa (2008, 207) finds that "identity contradictions are frequently
the manifestation of political conflicts at a personal level." According to Barvosa
(2008, 207), how people respond to identity contradictions has political
implications—some responses "are likely to perpetuate existing social and political
conflicts . . . [while others] have important implications for political participation
and for the potential for resolving ongoing political conflicts."

3. Similarly, Chhibber (2003, 421) finds that "women's [political] participation . . . depends upon their role in the household."

4. For a detailed discussion, see Weldon (2002, 2004); Htun and Weldon (2012); and
Han and Heldman (2017).

5. I draw from Michael Walzer's (1991, 302) neo-Tocquevillian argument, which finds that the strength of liberal democracy depends on a vibrant civil society. According to Chambers and Kymlicka (2002, 2), many scholars use a neo-Tocquevillian perspective "to analyze the strength of liberal democracy in the West, as well as the processes of democratization around the world." For a critique of Walzer's neo-Tocquevillian argument, see Rai (1994).

6. I. J. Singh (1998, 136) argues that "every Sikh can recite the hymn from the morning prayers which clearly reminds the follower that all are born of woman, that without her no one can exist, and then asks the rhetorical question: 'Why should one demean a woman?'"

7. Nikky Guninder Kaur Singh uses two different terms in her translation of this particular word. In *The Feminine Principle in the Sikh Vision of the Transcendent* (1993) she uses the word "inferior"; however, in "Female Feticide in the Punjab and Fetus Imagery in Sikhism" (2009) she uses "polluted." I include both.

8. This translation is from Nikky Singh (1993, 30; 2009, 125).

9. According to I. J. Singh (1998, 133), "Ask any Sikh, no matter how uninformed he or she is of Sikhism, of the place of women in Sikh teaching. The answer will be quick that they are equal. Ask any Sikh, no matter how liberated or erudite in the intricacies of the faith, on the position of women in Sikh society today and he or she will hem and haw, and side step the issue."

10. Singh's characterization of the British as champions of women's rights is problematic because, as Lata Mani (1987, 152) demonstrates, "Women are themselves marginal to the debate [on sati]." Similarly, Doris Jakobsh (2006, 183) finds that Sikh women were also marginal in the Singh Sabha reform movement: "Reformers of the late nineteenth and early twentieth centuries thought that women and the status of women could be transformed through a return to their respective 'golden ages,' ages that were increasingly legitimated through a rewriting of history, myth, and ritual. By and large, women themselves did not collaborate in these designs. Moreover, they were often portrayed as being opposed to their own liberation."

11. In chapter 5, I examine in more detail the role of Sukhmani Seva Societies in the Sikh community.

12. For a detailed discussion of my experience, see chapter 6.

13. According I. J. Singh (1998, 131), there is "no activity in the Sikh religion reserved exclusively for men, nor is there any which is closed to [women]."

14. "It is still very common and normal for a woman to progress over her life from being a daughter in her natal home, to a wife and daughter-in-law in her husband's and in-law's home, to a mother of young children, to a mother-in-law, and finally to an older woman, and frequently, a widow" (Mines and Lamb 2010, 75). For a detailed discussion, also see Nussbaum (2000); Mohanty (2003); Sangtin Writers and Nagar (2006).

15. Data on Indian women's educational attainment and labor market participation supports this claim: 65 percent of women are literate, compared to 82 percent of men; 26 percent of women complete secondary education, compared to 50 percent of men; and 33 percent of women participate in the labor market, compared to 81 percent of men (Rajivan 2010).

16. According to Chandra Mohanty (2003, 150), "The opposition between definitions of the 'laborer' and of the 'housewife' anchors the invisibility (and caste-related status) of work; in effect, it defines women as nonworkers."

17. According to Amrita Chhachhi, extreme forms of violence against women, such as dowry murders, police rape, abortion of female fetuses, and sati, can be connected to structural violence against women, including lack of property rights. For instance, Chhachhi (1989, 573) argues, "The issue of dowry murders is linked to the much more hidden and more widespread issue of violence within the family and the fact that women do not assert their right to property."

18. For a detailed discussion, see Agarwal (1994); Unni (1999); Kapadia (2002); and Datta (2006).

19. At this point in the interview, Beena Kaur says to me, "Please don't take offense, but look at your sleeves." At the time, I was wearing a traditional *salwar kameez* with a *dupata* around my neck, not on my head, and my *kameez* had short sleeves— something Beena Kaur found inappropriate and shameful.

20. In the north Indian context, dowry creates the structural asymmetry between the two families, and the consequent burden of gift giving on the bride's family strengthens inequality. Property in marriage has a double meaning: (1) the in-marrying young woman is viewed as the property of her husband and conjugal family; and (2) marriage marks the unequal flow of goods and property from the bride's natal family to her married family. Also, it is important to note the communal aspect of dowry, which is not a one-time transaction, but rather a continual process. Ritual occasions, festivals, and religious events often result in more demands being made by the in-laws (Karlekar 2004, 319).

21. In "Son Preference and Its Effect on Fertility in India," the authors argue that three major factors that underlie son preference in India: (1) sons are the source of economic utility, (2) sons provide sociocultural utility, and (3) sons provide religious utility (Mutharayappa et al. 1997, 5). Gupta (1987, 81–82) finds that birth order has a significant effect on child mortality rates, specifically the mortality rate for girls: "The data on sex differentials in child mortality by birth order show a steep rise in the mortality of girls at birth order four and higher. . . . Fourth and higher births appear to be geared toward achieving the desired quota of boys. This finding provides clear evidence of the role of behavioral factors in raising the mortality of girls. It also indicates that the burden of excessive mortality falls most heavily on girls at higher birth orders."

22. Nussbaum (2002, 100–101) finds that "in India the problem of violence against women is compounded, often, by the low age of marriage and the lack of economic options for a woman with little or no education. The marriage of girls as young as four or six, although long since illegal, is a common reality, especially in some regions where it is traditional. Laws against it are not enforced, and it shapes a girl's life from birth, often discouraging her family from educating her."

23. Similarly, Joti Sekhon (2006, 107) finds that Indian women's effective political participation is limited by "patriarchal social structures and norms about a woman's proper place and appropriate behavior in society. These barriers include the responsibility of housework and child rearing, lack of education and knowledge,

economic constraints, fear of failure and ridicule, corruption, fear of character debasement and bringing shame to the family."

CHAPTER 5

1. Sukhmani Seva Societies are devotional religious organizations in which men and women promote the recitation of Sukhmani Sahib prayer.
2. Jakeet Singh (2015, 661) describes this tension as a false paradox that is created by mainstream feminist scholars who ask why some women actively uphold and maintain religious practices that further women's subordination. For Singh (2015, 661), the questions being advanced by mainstream feminist scholars require scrutiny because they implicitly or explicitly reveal the "modernism of many feminisms, with its disdain for custom, tradition, and religion, and its teleological conception of progress tied to secularization and the ultimate demise (or at least privatization) of religion."
3. Kelsy Burke (2012, 123) identifies the four types of agency among gender-traditional religious women: resistance agency, empowerment agency, instrumental agency, and compliant agency. For Burke this expanded understanding of agency allows scholars to move past false dichotomies that understand women as "either empowered or victimized, liberated or subordinated" (123).
4. I follow Saba Mahmood's (2005, 14–15) insistence that the capacity to act "is entailed not only in those acts that resist norms but also in the multiple ways in which one *inhabits* norms."
5. When asked about their formal political participation, some female research participants did, however, discuss their connections to and reliance on local municipal councils and village panchayats to provide resources in their struggle to create Sukhmani Seva Societies. But participants did not discuss formal political engagement beyond these local institutions.
6. There is no English-language research conducted on Sukhmani Seva Societies and therefore there is no scholarly literature to cite. For example, there is no information on how many coed organizations exist in Punjab or in India. There is also no information about the number of all-female Sukhmani Seva Societies. Similarly, there is no information regarding the class, caste, and educational background of *sevadars* (volunteers or servants). Much of what I share is based on my own participant observation data and based on email correspondence with influential scholars of Sikh and Punjab studies. I would like to recognize and thank Shinder Thandi, Gurinder Singh Mann, Doris Jakobsh, and Eleanor Nesbitt for their email correspondence (August 2016).
7. Sukhmani Sahib is the name used to refer to a set of hymns from the Guru Granth Sahib (the Guru in book form), which outline major tenets of Sikhism through devotional poetic form (Guru Granth, 262–296). It was written by the fifth guru, Guru Arjan Dev. The word *sukh* means peace and the word *mani* means mind or heart. Thus, Sukhmani Sahib is often translated into English as Psalm or Song of Peace.
8. According to a *Tribune* article published on September 22, 2015, the Sukhmani Seva Society in Amritsar celebrated its fiftieth anniversary in Amritsar, Punjab, through a massive *nagar kirtan*.

9. *Chhabeel* is the free offering and distribution of a sweetened mixture of milk and water. *Chhabeel* is offered to everyone irrespective of his or her religious affiliation, caste and class background, and gender. Often *chhabeels* are organized to mark a significant event on the Sikh religious calendar, such as marking the birth, death, or martyrdom of a guru.

10. The SGPC is the legally authorized, democratically elected governing body of the Sikh community. The SGPC first came into being in response to the 1920s Gurdwara Reform Movement. The SGPC has managed and maintained historic *gurdwaras*, prepared a standard edition of the Guru Granth, developed an authoritative Sikh code of conduct (Rahit Marayada), and built schools and colleges.

11. *Gurdwara* has a metaphorical and empirical meaning. Metaphorically, the *gurdwara* is the *sangat* (congregation) itself, as Vahiguru is present whenever and wherever the *sangat* assembles. Empirically, the *gurdwara* is the physical space open to all, where the *sangat* assembles and is marked by the presence of Guru Granth, a *langar* hall, and *nishan sahib*. The *gurdwara* is also where *karah prasad* (blessed food) is distributed among the *sangat*. Lastly, *gurdwara* complexes provide residential quarters for pilgrims, libraries, and schools to teach Sikhism, history, *kirtan*, and *gurmukhi*.

12. Mata Khivi (1506–1582), the wife of the second guru, Guru Angad, was integral in the creation of the Sikh institution of *langar*.

13. Mata Gujri (1624–1705) was the wife of Guru Tegh Bahadur, the ninth guru of Sikhism, and the mother of Guru Gobind Singh, the tenth guru of Sikhism.

14. *Saropa* is one of the highest honors that a Sikh can receive in *sangat*. *Saropa* is a Persian term meaning head to foot. It is a single garment or a length of cloth given as a mark of piety, devotion, and philanthropy. It is usually two-and-a-half meters long and dyed saffron color.

15. Radhasoami is a religious community created in 1861 under the auspices of Swami Shiv Dayal Singh in Agra, India. Unlike Sikhs, Radhasoamis worship a living guru. Lower- and upper-caste Indians, Sikhs and Hindus, white Christians, and black South Africans are all included in the Radhasoami fold. Swami Shiv Dayal Singh's teachings "showed a mix of influences—Kabirpanthi, Sikh, Nath yogi, and Vaisnava—and focused on the efficacy of sacred words and the saving power of a spiritual master in transforming the self and achieving access to otherworldly realms" (Juergensmeyer 1991, 3). For a detailed discussion, see Juergensmeyer (1991).

16. Sagoo does not assume solidarity among women, but describes how religious difference, which initially divided the women, was overcome through divine agency: "In the beginning, women would come to the *gurdwara* when we met, but they wouldn't enter the *gurdwara*. They wanted to see the spectacle. You know, what's her name, Taro, Sukhwinder's wife, she and others used to come in the beginning. They would show up every week without fail, but they would sit outside and gossip, but they wouldn't join the prayers. I would always give them *prasad* (blessed food) and I would jokingly say to them, "Spend a little bit of your time praying inside and spend a little bit of your time gossiping outside." But at this point, these same women cooperate with me so much, very much so. I don't know how this change

came to be; Vahiguru made it happen; I don't know how it happened. Slowly, over time, the change occurs."

CHAPTER 6

1. Zenzele Isoke (2018, 155) describes this process in the following way: "The black ethnographer dives into the moldy crevices of erasure and finds breath. Inhaling, exhaling, listening, talking, sharing, creating. She resists suffocation. She is an artist."
2. For a detailed discussion, see Schwartz-Shea and Majic 2017.
3. Zenzele Isoke (2018, 163) argues that in political science "this form of expression forces us to pound our ideas into Cartesian formulations of objectivity, and to conceal our deepest intellectual impetus behind other people's words and other people's ideas. The 'I' is hidden behind the citation—the 'self' is shrouded in secrecy."
4. According to Peregrine Schwartz-Shea and Dvora Yanow (2012, 104), "Reflexivity enacts the systematicity of interpretive research in a manner that is consistent with an interpretive logic of inquiry."
5. Marsha Henry (2007, 71) argues that diasporic researchers have difficulties "positioning themselves . . . as authoritative agents in the field, especially when they find it difficult to make claims to 'authentic' places of 'origin' and 'pure' ethnic and racial identities."
6. For a detailed discussion, see Behl (2017a).
7. According to Mary Hawkesworth (2005, 141–142), political science fails to engage feminist scholarship: "Few doctoral programs allow students to develop areas of concentration in feminist approaches to political studies. Few routinely include feminist scholarship in proseminars in American politics, comparative politics, international relations, political theory, public law, or public policy. None requires familiarity with leading feminist scholarship as a criterion of professional competence." Hawkesworth (2005, 152) argues that by "refusing to read and engage feminist scholarship . . . political scientists violate the very norms of objectivity and systematicity that support the characterization of their own research as 'scientific.'" Similarly, J. Ann Tickner (2015, 549–550) argues that international relations scholarship is unwilling "to listen to new forms of critical thinking . . . [even though] our very survival may depend on being open to new ways of thinking." Likewise, Petra Ahrens et al. (2018, 8) critique "political science for its ongoing and unjust marginalisation and exclusion of knowledge produced by scholars in the fields of gender, sexuality and intersectionality. Too often, scholars are simply and straightforwardly excluded . . . other times, the process takes the subtler process of invisibilisation. Work and contributions are pushed aside, invalidated in some way or co-opted."

BIBLIOGRAPHY

Ackerly, Brooke. 2013. "Studying Politics in the Age of Academic Humility." *Politics, Groups, and Identities* 1 (1): 98–101.

Ackerly, Brooke. 2018. *Just Responsibility: A Human Rights Theory of Global Justice.* New York: Oxford Univeristy Press.

Ackerly, Brooke, and Jacqui True. 2010. *Doing Feminist Research in Political and Social Science.* New York: Palgrave Macmillan.

Ackerly, Brooke, and Jacqui True. 2013. "Methods and Methodologies." In *The Oxford University Handbook of Gender and Politics,* edited by Georgina Waylen, Karen Celis, Johanna Kantola, and S. Laurel Weldon, 135–159. Oxford: Oxford University Press.

Agarwal, Bina. 1994. *A Field of One's Own: Gender and Land Rights in South Asia.* Cambridge: Cambridge University Press.

Agnes, Flavia. 1996. "The Hidden Agenda beneath the Rhetoric of Women's Rights." In *The Nation, the State, and Indian Identity,* edited by Madhusree Dutta, Flavia Agnes, and Neera Adarkar, 68–94. Calcutta: Samya.

Agnes, Flavia. 1992. "Protecting Women against Violence? Review of a Decade of Legislation, 1980–89." *Economic and Political Weekly* 27 (17): WS-19–WS-33.

Ahrens, Petra, Karen Celis, Sarah Childs, Isabelle Engeli, Elizabeth Evans, and Liza Mugge. 2018. "Politics and Gender: Rocking Political Science and Creating New Horizons." *European Journal of Politics and Gender* 1 (1–2): 3–16.

Alcoff, Linda Martín. 2006. *Visible Identities: Race, Gender, and the Self.* Oxford: Oxford University Press.

Alexander-Floyd, Nikol. 2012. "Disappearing Acts: Reclaiming Intersectionality in the Social Sciences in a Post-Black Feminist Era." *Feminist Formations* 24 (1): 1–25.

Anzaldúa, Gloria. 1987. *Borderlands / La Frontera.* San Francisco: Spinster / Aunt Lute.

Anzaldúa, Gloria. 2003. "Speaking in Tongues: A Letter to Third World Women Writers." In *Women Writing Resistance: Essays on Latin American and the Caribbean,* edited by Jennifer Browdy de Hernandez, 79–90. Cambridge, MA: South End Press.

Anzaldúa, Gloria, and Cherríe Moraga. 1981. *This Bridge Called My Back: Writings by Radical Women of Color.* New York: Kitchen Table: Women of Color Press.

Atkinson, Rowland, and John Flint. 2001. "Accessing Hidden and Hard-to-Reach Populations: Snowball Research Strategies." *Social Research Update* 33 (Summer): 1–4.

Bagchi, Suvojit. 2013. "Women Equally Responsible for Crimes against Them." *The Hindu*, January 5, 2013. http://www.thehindu.com/news/national/women-equally-responsible-for-crimes-against-them/article4273827.ece.

Bajpai, Rochana. 2011. *Debating Difference: Groups Rights and Liberal Democracy in India*. New Delhi: Oxford University Press.

Baldwin, Katherine. 2012. "Canada Best G20 Country to Be a Woman, India Worst." Thomson Reuters, June 12, 2012. http://in.reuters.com/article/g20-women/canada-best-g20-country-to-be-a-woman-india-worst-idINDEE85C00420120613.

Banerjee, Sikakta. 2005. *Make Me a Man! Masculinity, Hinduism, and Nationalism in India*. Albany: State University of New York Press.

Banerjee, Sikakta. 2006. "Armed Masculinity, Hindu Nationalism and Female Political Participation in India: Heroic Mothers, Chaste Wives and Celibate Warriors." *International Feminist Journal of Politics* 8 (1): 62–83.

Banerjee, Sukanya, Angana Chatterji, Lunna Nazir Chaudhry, Manali Desai, Saadia Toor, and Kamala Visweswaran. 2004. "Engendering Violence: Boundaries, Histories, and the Everyday." *Cultural Dynamics* 16 (2–3): 125–139.

Banerjee-Patel, Tanvi and Rowena Robinson. 2017. "Inhabiting or Interrogating Faith: Piety among Muslim Women in Mumbai." *Economic & Political Weekly* 52 (42–43): 41–49.

Barvosa, Edwina. 2008. *Wealth of Selves: Multiple Identities, Mestiza Consciousness, and the Subject of Politics*. College Station: Texas A&M University Press.

Bassel, Leah, and Akwugo Emejulu. 2014. "Solidarity under Austerity: Intersectionality in France in the United Kingdom." *Politics & Gender* 10 (1): 130–136.

Bassel, Leah, and Eleonore Lepinard. 2014. "Introduction." *Politics & Gender* 10 (1): 115–117.

Basu, Moni. 2013. "The Girl Whose Rape Changed a Country." *CNN*, November 2013. http://www.cnn.com/interactive/2013/11/world/india-rape/

Baukje, Prins. 2006. "Mothers and Muslims, Sisters and Sojourners: The Contested Boundaries of Feminist Citizenship." In *Handbook of Gender and Women's Studies*, edited by Kathy Davis, Mary Evans, and Judith Lorber, 234–250. London: Sage Publications.

Baxi, Pratiksha. 2012. "Rape Cultures in India." *Outlook India*, December 23, 2012. http://www.outlookindia.com/website/story/rape-cultures-in-india/283776.

Baxi, Pratiksha. 2014. *Public Secrets of Law: Rape Trials in India*. New Delhi: Oxford University Press.

Baxi, Pratiksha, Shirin Rai, and Shaheen Sardar Ali. 2007. "Legacies of Common Law: 'Crimes of Honour' in India and Pakistan." *Third World Quarterly* 27 (7): 1239–1253.

Baxi, Upendra. 1982. *The Crisis in the Indian Legal System*. New Delhi: Vikas.

Bayard de Volo, Lorraine, and Edward Schatz. 2004. "From the Inside Out: Ethnographic Methods in Political Research." *PS: Political Science & Politics* 37: 267–271.

Beer, Caroline. 2009. "Democracy and Gender Equality." *Studies in Comparative International Development* 44 (3): 212–227.

Behl, Natasha. 2009. "Uniformities and Differences of a Sikh Nationalist Identity: Opinions and Practices of Ordinary Sikhs." *Journal of Punjab Studies* 16 (2): 199–217.

Behl, Natasha. 2010. "Politics of Equality: Caste and Gender Paradoxes in the Sikh Community." PhD dissertation, University of California, Los Angeles.

Behl, Natasha. 2012. "Sikh Minority Identity Formation." In *Minority Studies*, edited by Rowena Robinson, 249–269. Delhi: Oxford University Press.

Behl, Natasha. 2014. "Situated Citizenship: Understanding Sikh Citizenship through Women's Exclusion." *Politics, Groups, and Identities* 2 (3): 386–401.

Behl, Natasha. 2017a. "Diasporic Researcher: An Autoethnographic Analysis of Gender and Race in Political Science." *Politics, Groups, and Identities* 5 (4): 580–598.

Behl, Natasha. 2017b. "Gendered Discipline, Gendered Space: An Ethnographic Approach to Gendered Violence in India." *Space & Polity* 21 (1): 43–58.

Behl, Natasha. 2019. "Mapping Movements and Motivations: An Autoethnographic Analysis of Racial, Gendered, and Epistemic Violence in Academia." *Feminist Formations* 31 (1): 85–102.

Bell, Derrick. 1980. "Brown v. Board of Education and the Interest-Convergence Dilemma." *Harvard Law Review* 93 (3): 518–553.

Beltran, Cristina. 2010. *The Trouble with Unity: Latino Politics and the Creation of Identity*. Oxford: Oxford University Press.

Bhalla, Nita. 2012. "India Advances, but Many Women Still Trapped in Dark Ages." Thomson Reuters Foundation, June 13, 2012. http://news.trust.org/item/20120613010100-b7scy/?source=spotlight.

Bhalla, Nita. 2013. "What Stopped India's 'Anti-rape' Law from Being a Landmark?" Reuters, March 28, 2013. http://news.trust.org//item/20130328133800-yns12/.

Bhatt, Abhinav. 2013. "'Women Meant to Do Household Chores': Another Shocker from RSS Chief." *NDTV*, January 6, 2013. http://www.ndtv.com/article/india/women-meant-to-do-household-chores-another-shockerfrom-rss-chief-313779.

Bhavani, Kum-Kum, John Foran, Priya A. Kurian, and Debashish Munshi. 2016. *Feminist Futures: Reimagining Women, Culture and Development*. London: Zed Books.

Bilge, Sirma. 2010. "Beyond Subordination vs. Resistance: An Intersectional Approach to the Agency of Veiled Muslim Women." *Journal of Intercultural Studies* 31 (1): 9–28.

Bilge, Sirma. 2013a. "Intersectionality Undone: Saving Intersectionality from Feminist Intersectionality Studies." *Du Bois Review* 10 (2): 405–424.

Bilge, Sirma. 2013b. "Whitening Intersectionality: Evanescence of Race in Intersectionality Scholarship." In *Racism and Sociology*, edited by W. D. Hund and A. Lentin, 175–206. Berlin: Lit Verlag.

Bonilla-Silva, Eduardo, and Tukufu Zuberi. 2008. *White Logic, White Methods: Racism and Methodology*. Lanham, MD: Rowman & Littlefield.

Booth, Beverley, and Manorama Verma. 1992. "Decreased Access to Medical Care for Girls in Punjab, India: The Roles of Age, Religion, and Distance." *American Journal of Public Health* 82 (8): 1155–1157.

Bosco, Dominiquel. 2013. "Pondy Solution to Rape: Hide Girls under Overcoats." *Times of India*, January 6, 2013. http://timesofindia.indiatimes.com/city/chennai/Pondy-solution-to-rape-Hide-girls-under-overcoats/articleshow/17908055.cms.

Bracke, Sarah. 2003. "Author(iz)ing Agency: Feminist Scholars Making Sense of Women's Involvement in Religious 'Fundamentalist' Movements." *European Journal of Women's Studies* 10 (3): 335–46.

Brah, Avtar. 2005. "Locality, Globality and Gendered Refractions." *Punjab Studies Journal* 12 (1): 153–165.

Brah, Avtar, and Ann Phoenix. 2004. "Ain't I a Woman? Revisiting Intersectionality." *Journal of International Women's Study* 5 (3): 75–86.

Brodkin, Evelyn Z. 2017. "The Ethnographic Turn in Political Science: Reflections on the State of the Art." *PS: Political Science & Politics* 50 (1): 131–134.

Brown, Michael, Martin Carnoy, Elliott Currie, Troy Duster, David Oppenheimer, Marjorie Shultz, and David Wellman. 2003. *White Washing Race: The Myth of a Color-Blind Society*. Berkeley: University of California Press.

Brown, Nadia. 2014. *Sisters in the Statehouse: Black Women and Legislative Decision Making*. Oxford: Oxford University Press.

Brubaker, Rogers. 2004. *Ethnicity without Groups*. Cambridge, MA: Harvard University Press.

Bucar, Elizabeth M. 2010. "Dianomy: Understanding Religious Women's Moral Agency as Creative Conformity." *Journal of the American Academy of Religion* 78 (3): 662–86.

Burke, Kelsy C. 2012. "Women's Agency in Gender-Traditional Religions: A Review of Four Approaches." *Sociology Compass* 6 (2): 122–33.

Campbell, Andrea Louise. 2014. *Trapped in America's Safety Net: One Family's Struggle*. Chicago: University of Chicago Press.

Campbell, Andrea Louise. 2015. "Family Story as Political Science: Reflections on Writing Trapped in America's Safety Net." *Perspectives on Politics* 13 (4): 1043–1052.

Caraway, Teri. 2004. "Inclusion and Democratization: Class, Gender, Race, and the Extensions of Suffrage." *Comparative Politics* 36 (4): 443–460.

Chakrabarty, Dipesh. 2000. *Provincializing Europe: Postcolonial Thought and Historical Difference*. Princeton, NJ: Princeton University Press.

Chambers, Simone, and Will Kymlicka. 2002. "Introduction: Alternative Conceptions of Civil Society." In *Alternative Conceptions of Civil Society*, edited by Simone Chambers and Will Kymlicka, 1–10. Princeton, NJ: Princeton University Press.

Chappell, Louise. 2014. "Conflicting Institutions and the Search for Gender Justice at the International Criminal Court." *Political Research Quarterly* 67 (1): 183–196.

Chatterji, Angana. 1990. "Women in Search of Human Equality." *Social Action* 40 (1): 46–57.

Chatterji, Angana, Shashi Buluswar, and Mallika Kaur. 2015. *Conflicted Democracies and Gendered Violence: The Right to Heal*. Berkeley, CA: BerkeleyHaas.

Chhachhi, Amrita. 1989. "The State, Religious Fundamentalism and Women: Trends in South Asia." *Economic and Political Weekly* 24 (11): 567–578.

Chhibber, Pradeep. 2003. "Why Some Women Are Politically Active: The Household, Public Space, and Political Participation in India." *International Journal of Comparative Sociology* 43: 409–429.

Chong, Kelly H. 2008. "Coping with Conflict, Confronting Resistance: Fieldwork Emotions and Identity Management in a South Korean Evangelical Community." *Qualitative Sociology* 31 (4): 369–390.

CIA World Factbook. 2012. "Sex Ratio." https://www.cia.gov/library/publications/the-world-factbook/fields/2018.html.

Cohn, Carol. 1987. "Sex and Death in the Rational World of Defense Intellectuals." *Signs* 12: 687–718.

Collins, Patricia Hill. 1986. "Learning from the Outsider Within: The Sociological Significance of Black Feminist Thought." *Social Problems* 33 (6): S14–S32.

Collins, Patricia Hill. 1989. "The Social Construction of Black Feminist Thought." *Signs* 14 (4): 745–773.

Collins, Patricia Hill. 1990. *Black Feminist Thought: Knowledge, Consciousness, and the Politics of Empowerment.* Boston: Unwin Hyman.

Collins, Patricia Hill, and Valerie Chepp. 2013. "Intersectionality." In *The Oxford University Handbook of Gender and Politics,* edited by Georgina Waylen, Karen Celis, Johanna Kantola, and S. Laurel Weldon, 57–87. Oxford: Oxford University Press.

Combahee River Collective. [1977] 1997. "A Black Feminist Statement." In *The Second Wave: A Reader in Feminist Theory,* edited by Linda Nicolson, 63–70. New York: Routledge.

Cramer, Renee Ann. 2005. *Cash, Color, and Colonialism: The Politics of Tribal Acknowledgment.* Norman: University of Oklahoma Press.

Crenshaw, Kimberlé. 1989. "Demarginalizing the Intersection of Race and Sex: A Black Feminist Critique of Antidiscrimination Doctrine, Feminist Theory and Antiracist Politics." *University of Chicago Legal Forum 1989* (1): 139–67.

Crenshaw, Kimberlé. 1991. "Mapping the Margins: Intersectionality, Identity Politics, and Violence against Women of Color." *Stanford Law Review* 43 (6): 1241–1299.

Crenshaw, Kimberlé. 1995. "Introduction." In *Critical Race Theory: The Key Writings That Formed the Movement,* edited by Kimberlé Crenshaw, Neil Gotanda, Gary Peller, and Kendall Thomas, xiii–xxxii. New York: New Press.

Crowley, Helen, Gail Lewis, Pnina Werbner, and Nira Yuval-Davis. 1997. "Citizenship: Pushing the Boundaries." *Feminist Review* 57 (Autumn): 1–3.

Das, Veena. 1999. "Communities as Political Actors: The Question of Cultural Rights." In *Gender and Politics in India,* edited by Nivedita Menon, 441–471. Oxford: Oxford University Press.

Das, Veena. 2007. *Life and Words: Violence and the Descent into the Ordinary.* Berkeley: University of California Press.

Das, Veena, and Shalini Randeria. 2014. "Democratic Strivings, Social Sciences, and Public Debates: The Case of India." *American Anthropologist* 116 (1): 160–172.

Datta, Ayona. 2016. "The Intimate City: Violence, Gender and Ordinary Life in Delhi Slums." *Urban Geography* 37 (3): 323–342.

Datta, Namita. 2006. "Joint Titling—a Win-Win Policy? Gender and Property Rights in Urban Informal Settlements in Chandigarh, India." *Feminist Economics* 12 (1–2): 271–298.

Dauphinee, Elizabeth. 2010. "The Ethics of Autoethnography." *Review of International Studies* 36 (3): 799–818.

Delgado, Richard. 1984. "The Imperial Scholar: Reflections on a Review of Civil Rights Literature." *University of Pennsylvania Law Review* 132 (3): 561–578.

Deol, Harnik. 2000. *Religion and Nationalism in India: The Case of Punjab*. New York: Routledge.

Dhami, M. S. 1995. "Caste, Class and Politics in Rural Punjab: A Study of two Villages in Sangrur District." In *The Story of Punjab Yesterday and Today, vol. 2*, edited by Verinder Grover, 49–70. Delhi: Deep & Deep Publications.

Dhamoon, Rita. 2011. "Considerations on Mainstreaming Intersectionality." *Political Research Quarterly* 64 (1): 230–243.

Dhamoon, Rita. 2013. "Feminisms." In *The Oxford University Handbook of Gender and Politics*, edited by Georgina Waylen, Karen Celis, Johanna Kantola, and S. Laurel Weldon, 88–110. Oxford: Oxford University Press.

Doty, Roxanne Lynn. 2004. "Maladies of Our Souls: Identity and Voice in the Writing of Academic International Relations." *Cambridge Review of International Affairs* 17 (2): 377–392.

Dutta, Anup. 2014. "Chennai Women More Religious So Sexual Crimes Are Lower: Babulal Gaur's New Gem." *India Today*, January 11, 2014. http://indiatoday.intoday.in/story/mp-minister-babulal-gaur-links-women-attire-to-crimes/1/335615.html.

Eisenberg, Ann Marie. 2011. "Law on the Books vs. Law in Action: Under-enforcement of Morocco's Reformed 2004 Family Law, the Moudawana." *Cornell International Law Journal* 44 (3): 693–728.

Elman, R. Amy. 2013. "Gender Violence." In *The Oxford University Handbook of Gender and Politics*, edited by Georgina Waylen, Karen Celis, Johanna Kantola, and S. Laurel Weldon, 236–258. Oxford: Oxford University Press.

Embree, Ainslie. 1990. *Utopias in Conflict: Religion and Nationalism in Modern India*. Berkeley: University of California Press.

Feminist Review. 1984. "Many Voices, One Chant: Black Feminist Perspectives." *Feminist Review* 17.

Fenno, Richard. 1978. *Home Style: House Members in their Districts*. Pearson College Division.

Finifter, Ada. 1983. *Political Science: The State of the Discipline*. Washington, DC: American Political Science Association.

Forbath, William. 1999. "Caste, Class, and Equal Citizenship." *Michigan Law Review* 98 (1): 1–91.

Forrest, M. David. 2017. "Engaging and Disrupting Power: The Public Value of Political Ethnography." *PS: Political Science & Politics* 50 (1): 109–113.

Fujji, Lee Ann. 2018. *Interviewing in Social Science Research: A Relational Approach*. New York: Routledge.

Ganguly, Sumit. 2003. "The Crisis of Indian Secularism." *Journal of Democracy* 14 (4): 11–25.

Geddes, Barbara. 2003. *Paradigms and Sand Castles: Theory Building and Research Design in Comparative Politics*. Ann Arbor: University of Michigan Press.

Glenn, Evelyn Nakano. 2000. "Citizenship and Inequality: Historical and Global Perspectives." *Social Problems* 47 (1): 1–20.

Glenn, Evelyn Nakano. 2002. *Unequal Freedom: How Race and Gender Shaped American Citizenship and Labor*. Cambridge, MA: Harvard University Press.

Glenn, Evelyn Nakano. 2011. "Constructing Citizenship: Exclusion, Subordination, and Resistance." *American Sociological Review* 76 (1): 2–25.

Gomez, Laura. 2000. "Race, Colonialism, and Criminal Law: Mexicans and the American Criminal Justice System in Territorial New Mexico." *Law and Society Review* 34 (4): 1129–1202.

Gomez, Laura. 2008. *Manifest Destinies: The Making of the Mexican American Race.* New York: New York University Press.

Greenstein, Fred, and Nelson Polsby. 1975. *Handbook of Political Science*, vols. 1–7. Reading, MA: Addison-Wesley.

Grewal, Inderpal, and Caren Kaplan. 1994. *Scattered Hegemonies: Postmodernity and Transnational Feminist Practices.* Minneapolis: University of Minnesota Press.

Grewal, J. S. 1990. *The Sikhs of the Punjab.* New York: Cambridge University Press.

Grewal, Jyoti. 2008. "Theorizing Activism, Activizing Theory: Feminist Academics in Indian Punjabi Society." *NWSA Journal* 20 (1): 161–183.

Guha, Ranajit. 1988. "On Some Aspects of the Historiography of Colonial India." In *Selected Subaltern Studies*, edited by Ranajit Guha and Gayatri Chakravorty Spivak, 37–44. Oxford: Oxford University Press.

Guha, Ranajit, and Gayatri Chakravorty Spivak, eds. 1988. *Selected Subaltern Studies.* Oxford: Oxford University Press.

Gupta, Monica Das. 1987. "Selective Discrimination against Female Children in Rural Punjab, India." *Population Development Review* 13 (1): 77–100.

Hall, Stuart, and David Held. 1990. "Citizens and Citizenship." In *New Times*, edited by Stuart Hall and Jacques Martin, 173–188. New York: Verso.

Hall, Tom, and Howard Williamson. 1999. *Citizenship and Community.* Leicester: Youth Work Press.

Han, Lori Cox, and Caroline Heldman. *Women, Power, and Politics: The Fight for Gender Equality in the United States.* New York: Oxford University Press.

Hanchard, Michael. 2006. *Party/Politics: Horizons in Black Political Thought.* Oxford: Oxford University Press.

Hancock, Ange-Marie. 2007a. "Intersectionality as a Normative and Empirical Paradigm." *Politics and Gender* 3 (2): 248–254.

Hancock, Ange-Marie. 2007b. "When Multiplication Doesn't Equal Quick Addition." *Perspectives on Politics* 5 (1): 63–79.

Hancock, Ange-Marie. 2016. *Intersectionality: An Intellectual History.* Oxford: Oxford University Press.

Hancock, Ange-Marie, and Evelyn Simien. 2011. "Mini-symposium: Intersectionality and Public Research." *Political Research Quarterly* 64 (1): 185–186.

Hankivsky, Olena, and Renee Cormier. 2011. "Intersectionality and Public Policy: Some Lessons from Existing Models." *Political Research Quarterly* 64 (1): 217–229.

Harding, Sandra. 1986. *The Science Question in Feminism.* Ithaca, NY: Cornell University Press.

Haritaworn, Jin, Adi Kuntsman, and Silvia Posocco. 2013. "Murderous Inclusions." *International Feminist Journal of Politics* 15 (4): 445–452.

Harris, Angela. 1990. "Race and Essentialism in Feminist Legal Theory." *Stanford Law Review* 42 (3): 581–616.

Hassim, Shireen. 2018. "Decolonising Equality: the Radical Roots of the Gender Equality Clause in the South African Constitution." *South African Journal on Human Rights* 34 (3): 342–358.

Hawkesworth, Mary. 2005. "Engendering Political Science: An Immodest Proposal." *Politics & Gender* 1 (1): 141–156.

Hawkesworth, Mary. 2006a. *Feminist Inquiry: From Political Conviction to Methodological Innovation*. New Brunswick, NJ: Rutgers University Press.

Hawkesworth, Mary. 2006b. "Contending Conceptions of Science and Politics: Methodology and the Constitutions of the Political." In *Interpretation and Method: Empirical Research Methods and the Interpretive Turn*, edited by Dvora Yanow and Peregrine Schwartz-Shea, 27–49. Armonk, NY: M.E. Sharpe.

Hawkesworth, Mary. 2013. "Sex, Gender, and Sexuality: From Naturalized Presumption to Analytical Categories." In *The Oxford University Handbook of Gender and Politics*, edited by Georgina Waylen, Karen Celis, Johanna Kantola, and S. Laurel Weldon, 31–56. Oxford: Oxford University Press.

Held, David. 1991. "Between State and Civil Society: Citizenship." In *Citizenship*, edited by Geoff Andrews, 19–25. London: Lawrence & Wishart.

Henderson, Frances. 2009. "'We Thought You Would Be White': Race and Gender in Fieldwork." *PS: Political Science & Politics* 42 (2): 291–294.

Henry, Marsha. 2007. "If the Shoe Fits: Authenticity, Authority, and Agency Feminist Diasporic Research." *Women's Studies International Forum* 30 (1): 70–80.

Hirsi Ali, Ayaan. 2006. *The Caged Virgin: An Emancipation Proclamation for Women and Islam*. New York: Free Press.

Hobsbawm, Eric. 1980. *Peasants in History: Essays in Honour of Daniel Thorner*. Calcutta: Oxford University Press.

Hochstetler, Kathryn, and Manjana Milkoreit. 2014. "Emerging Powers in the Climate Negotiations: Shifting Identity Conceptions." *Political Research Quarterly* 67 (1): 224–235.

Hodge, Amanda. 2013. "Caste Skews India's View of Rape." *The Australian*, August 30, 2013. http://www.theaustralian.com.au/news/world/caste-skewsindias-view-of-rape/story-e6frg6so-1226706934297.

hooks, bell. 1981. *Ain't I a Woman: Black Women and Feminism*. Boston: South End Press.

hooks, bell. 1994. *Teaching to Transgress: Education as the Practice of Freedom*. New York: Routledge.

Htun, Mala, and S. Laurel Weldon. 2010. "When Do Governments Promote Women's Rights? A Framework for the Comparative Analysis of Sex Equality Policy." *Perspectives on Politics* 8 (1): 207–216.

Htun, Mala, and S. Laurel Weldon. 2011. "State Power, Religion, and Women's Rights: A Comparative Analysis of Family Law." *Indiana Journal of Global Legal Studies* 18 (1): 145–165.

Htun, Mala, and S. Laurel Weldon. 2012. "The Civic Origins of Progressive Policy Change: Combating Violence against Women in Global Perspective, 1975–2005." *American Political Science Review* 106 (3): 548–569.

Human Rights Watch. 2012. "India: Rape Victim's Death Demands Action: Reform Sexual Assault Laws, Treatment of Survivors." Human Rights Watch, December 29, 2012. http://www.hrw.org/news/2012/12/29/india-rape-victim-s-death-demands-action.

Hume, Mo and Polly Wilding. 2019. "Beyond Agency and Passivity: Situating a Gendered Articulation of Urban Violence in Brazil and El Salvador." *Urban Studies* (In Press).

Ikegame, Aya. 2012. "Mathas, Gurus and Citizenship: The State and Communities in Colonial India." *Citizenship Studies* 16 (5–6): 689–703.

Indian Census. 2011a. "Distribution of Population by Religions."

Indian Census. 2011b. "Gender Composition."

Indian Census. 2011c. "Punjab Population Data."

Isin, Engin. 2002. "Citizenship after Orientalism." In *Handbook of Citizenship Studies,* edited by Engin Isin and B. S. Turner, 117–128. London: Sage.

Isin, Engin. 2008. "Theorizing Acts of Citizenship." In *Acts of Citizenship,* edited by Engin Isin and G. M. Nielsen, 15–43. London: Palgrave Macmillan.

Isin, Engin. 2011. "Ottoman Waqfs as Acts of Citizenship." In *Held in Trust: Waqf in the Muslim World,* edited by P. Ghazaleh, 209–229. Cairo: American University in Cairo Press.

Isin, Engin. 2012. "Citizenship after Orientalism: An Unfinished Project." *Citizenship Studies* 15 (5–6): 563–572.

Isin, Engin, and Ebru Ustundag. 2008. "Wills, Deeds, Acts: Women's Civic Gift-Giving in Ottoman Istanbul." *Gender, Place and Culture* 15 (5): 519–532.

Islam, Naheed. 2000. "Research as an Act of Betrayal: Researching Race in an Asian Community in Los Angeles." In *Racing Research, Researching Race: Methodological Dilemmas in Critical Race Studies,* edited by France Winddance Twine and Jonathan Warren, 35–66. New York: New York University Press.

Isoke, Zenzele. 2018. "Black Ethnography, Black(Female)Aesthetics: Thinking/Writing/ Saying/Sounding Black Political Life." *Theory & Event* 21 (1): 148–168.

Jakobsh, Doris. 2000. "The Construction of Gender in History and Religion: The Sikh Case." In *Faces of the Feminine in Ancient, Medieval, and Modern India,* edited by Mandakranta Bose, 270–286. Oxford: Oxford University Press.

Jakobsh, Doris. 2003. *Relocating Gender in Sikh History: Transformation, Meaning and Identity.* Oxford: Oxford University Press.

Jakobsh, Doris. 2006. "Sikhism, Interfaith Dialogue, and Women: Transformation and Identity." *Journal of Contemporary Religion* 21 (2): 183–199.

Jha, Prabhat, Rajesh Kumar, Priya Vasa, Neeraj Dhingra, Deva Thiruchelvam, and Rahim Moineddin. 2006. "Low Male-to-Female Sex Ratio of Children Born in India: National Survey of 1.1 Million Households." *The Lancet* 367 (9506): 211–218.

Jodhka, Surinder S. 2004. "Dissociation, Distancing and Autonomy: Caste and Untouchability in Rural Punjab." In *Dalits in Regional Context,* edited by Harish Puri, 62–99. Delhi: Rawat.

John, Mary. 1996. *Discrepant Dislocations: Feminism, Theory, and Postcolonial Histories.* Berkeley: University of California Press.

Jordan-Zachery, Julia. 2007. "Am I a Black Woman or a Woman Who Is Black? A Few Thoughts on the Meaning of Intersectionality." *Politics & Gender* 3 (2): 254–263.

Juergensmeyer, Mark. 1991. *Radhasoami Reality: The Logic of a Modern Faith*. Princeton, NJ: Princeton University Press.

Kabeer, Naila. 2015. "Grief and Rage in India: Making Violence against Women History?" Open Democracy, March 5, 2015. https://www.opendemocracy.net/5050/naila-kabeer/grief-and-rage-in-india-making-violence-against-women-history.

Kale, Priya. 2013. "Stalling a Paradigm Shift? The Official Response to the Justice Verma Committee Report." London School of Economics and Political Science, February 13, 2013. http://blogs.lse.ac.uk/indiaatlse/2013/02/13/stalling-a-paradigm-shift/.

Kapadia, Kiran. 2002. *The Violence of Development: The Politics of Identity, Gender, and Social Inequalities in India*. New Delhi: Kali for Women.

Kapur, Ratna. 2002. "The Tragedy of Victimization Rhetoric: Resurrecting the Native Subject in International/Postcolonial Feminist Legal Politics." *Harvard Human Rights Law Journal* 15 (1): 1–37.

Kapur, Ratna. 2007. "Challenging the Liberal Subject: Law and Gender Justice in South Asia." In *Gender Justice, Citizenship and Development*, edited by Maitrayee Mukhopadhyay and Navsharan Singh, 116–170. New Delhi: Zubaan, an imprint of Kali for Women and International Development Research Centre.

Kapur, Ratna, and Brenda Cossman. 1999. "On Women, Equality and the Constitution: through the Looking Glass of Feminism." In *Gender and Politics in India*, edited by Nivedita Menon, 197–261. Oxford: Oxford University Press.

Karlekar, Malavika. 2004. "Domestic Violence." In *Handbook of Indian Sociology*, edited by Veena Das, 308–330. New Delhi: Oxford University Press.

Kaur, Upinder Jit. 1990. *Sikh Religion and Economic Development*. New Delhi: National Book Organisation.

Keating, Christine. 2007. "Framing the Postcolonial Sexual Contract: Democracy, Fraternalism, and State Authority in India." *Hypatia* 22 (4): 130–145.

Keating, Christine. 2011. *Decolonizing Democracy: Transforming the Social Contract in India*. University Park: Pennsylvania State University.

Kelley, Robin D. G. 1994. *Race Rebels: Culture, Politics, and the Black Working Class*. New York: Free Press.

King, Deborah. 1988. "Multiple Jeopardy, Multiple Consciousness: The Context of a Black Feminist Ideology." *Signs* 14: 42–72.

King, Gary, Robert Keohane, and Sidney Verba. 1994. *Designing Social Inquiry*. Princeton, NJ: Princeton University Press.

Kymlicka, Will. 1995. *Multicultural Citizenship: A Liberal Theory of Minority Rights*. Cambridge: Cambridge University Press.

Kymlicka, Will, and Wayne Norman. 1994. "Return of the Citizen: A Survey of Recent Work on Citizenship Theory." *Ethics* 104 (2): 352–381.

Lee, Taeku. 2008. "Race, Immigration, and the Identity-to-Politics Link." *Annual Review of Political Science* 11: 457–478.

Lepinard, Eleonore. 2014. "Impossible Intersectionality? French Feminists and the Struggle for Inclusion." *Politics & Gender* 10 (1): 124–130.

Lister, Ruth. 1997a. "Citizenship: Towards a Feminist Synthesis." *Feminist Review* 57: 28–48.

Lister, Ruth. 1997b. *Citizenship: Feminist Perspectives*. London: Macmillan.

Lister, Ruth. 2007. "Inclusive Citizenship: Realizing the Potential." *Citizenship Studies* 11 (1): 49–61.

Lister, Ruth, Fiona Williams, Annelis Anttonen, Jet Bussemaker, Ute Gerhard, Jacqueline Heinen, Stina Johansson, Arnlaug Leira, Birte Siim, and Constanza Tobio. 2007. *Gendering Citizenship in Western Europe: New Challenges for Citizenship Research in a Cross-National Context*. Bristol: Policy Press.

Lodhia, Sharmila. 2015. "From 'Living Corpse' to India's Daughter: Exploring the Social, Political and Legal Landscape of the 2012 Delhi Gang Rape." *Women's Studies International Forum* 50: 89–101.

Lopez, Ian Haney. 2006. *White by Law: The Legal Construction of Race*. New York: New York University Press.

Mahmood, Saba. 2005. *Politics of Piety: The Islamic Revival and the Feminist Subject*. Princeton, NJ: Princeton University Press.

Mandair, Navdeep. 2005. "(EN)Gendered Sikhism: The Iconolatry of Manliness in the Making of Sikh Identity." *Sikh Formations* 1 (1): 39–55.

Mandhana, Niharika, and Anjan Trivedi. 2012. "Indians Outraged over Rape on Moving Bus in New Delhi." *New York Times*, December 18, 2012. http://india.blogs.nytimes.com/2012/12/18/outrage-in-delhi-after-latest-gang-rape-case/.

Mani, Lata. 1987. "Contentious Traditions: The Debate on Sati in Colonial India." *Cultural Critique* 7: 119–156.

Mani, Lata. 1990. "Multiple Mediations: Feminist Scholarship in the Age of Multinational Reception." *Feminist Review* 35 (Summer): 24–91.

Mann, Gurinder Singh. 2001. *The Making of Sikh Scriptures*. Oxford: Oxford University Press.

Mann, Gurinder Singh. 2004. *Sikhism*. Upper Saddle River, NJ: Prentice Hall.

Mann, Gurinder Singh. 2006. "The Sikh Community." In *The Oxford Handbook of Global Religions*, edited by Mark Juergensmeyer, 41–50. New York: Oxford University Press.

Marshall, T. H. 1950. *Citizenship and Social Class*. Cambridge: Cambridge University Press.

Marshall, T. H. 1964. *Class, Citizenship, and Social Development*. Garden City, NY: Doubleday and Company.

Matsuda, Mari. [1988] 1992. "When the First Quail Calls: Multiple Consciousness as Jurisprudential Method." *Women's Rights Law Reporter* 14 (2–3): 297–300.

McLeod, W. H. 1975. *The Evolution of the Sikh Community: Five Essays*. Delhi: Oxford University Press.

McLeod, W. H. 1989. *Who Is a Sikh? The Problem of Sikh Identity*. Oxford: Clarendon Press.

McLeod, W. H. 1995. *Historical Dictionary of Sikhism*. Lanham, MD: Scarecrow Press.

Menjivar, Cecilia. 2011. *Enduring Violence: Ladina Women's Lives in Guatemala*. Berkeley: University of California Press.

Menon, Kalyani. 2010. *Everyday Nationalism: Women of the Hindu Right in India*. Philadelphia: University of Pennsylvania Press.

Menon, Nivedita. 1999a. "Rights, Bodies and the Law: Rethinking Feminist Politics of Justice." In *Gender and Politics in India*, edited by Nivedita Menon, 262–295. Oxford: Oxford University Press.

Menon, Nivedita. 1999b. "Introduction." In *Gender and Politics in India*, edited by Nivedita Menon, 1–36. Oxford: Oxford University Press.

Menon, Nivedita. 2004. *Recovering Subversion: Feminist Politics beyond the Law*. Urbana: University of Illinois Press.

Merry, Sally Engle. [1988] 1992. "Rights Talk and the Experience of Law: Implementing Women's Human Rights to Protection from Violence." *Human Rights Quarterly* 25 (2): 343–381.

Merry, Sally Engle. 2000. *Colonizing Hawai'i: The Cultural Power of Law*. Princeton, NJ: Princeton University Press.

Merry, Sally Engle. 2009. *Gender Violence: A Cultural Perspective*. Malden, MA: Wiley-Blackwell.

Mignolo, Walter. 2006. "Citizenship, Knowledge, and the Limits of Humanity." *American Literary History* 18 (2): 312–331.

Miller, Barbara. 1981. *The Endangered Sex: Neglect of Female Children in Rural North India*. Ithaca, NJ: Cornell University Press.

Mills, Charles. 1999. *The Racial Contract*. Ithaca, NJ: Cornell University Press.

Mines, Diane, and Sarah Lamb. 2010. *Everyday Life in South Asia*. Bloomington: Indiana University Press.

Mohanty, Chandra. 2003. *Feminism without Borders: Decolonizing Theory, Practicing Solidarity*. Durham, NC: Duke University Press.

Modiri, Joel. 2018. "Introduction to Special Issue: Conquest, Constitutionalism, and Democratic Contestations." *South African Journal on Human Rights* 34 (3): 295–299.

Mouffe, Chantal. 1992. *Dimensions of Democracy*. London: Verso.

Mutharayappa, Rangamuthia, Minja Kim Choe, Fred Arnold, and T. K. Roy. 1997. "Son Preference and Its Effect on Fertility in India." *National Family Health Survey Subject Reports* 3: 3–35.

Nagar, Richa, and Susan Geiger. 2007. "Reflexivity and Positionality in Feminist Fieldwork Revisited." In *Politics and Practice in Economic Geography*, edited by Adam Tickell, Eric Sheppard, Jamic Peck, and Trevor Barnes, 267–278. Thousand Oaks, CA: Sage.

Narayan, Uma. 1997. *Dislocating Cultures: Identities, Traditions, and Third World Feminism*. New York: Routledge.

Neveu, Catherine. 2015. "Of Ordinariness and Citizenship Processes." *Citizenship Studies* 19 (2): 141–154.

Nussbaum, Martha. 2000. *Women and Human Development: The Capabilities Approach*. Cambridge: Cambridge University Press.

Nussbaum, Martha. 2001. "India: Implementing Sex Equality through Law." *Chicago Journal of International Law* 2 (1): 35–58.

Nussbaum, Martha. 2002. "Sex, Laws, and Inequality: What India Can Teach the United State." *Daedalus* 131 (1): 95–106.

Okin, Susan. 1979. *Women in Western Political Thought*. Princeton, NJ: Princeton University Press.

Okin Susan Moller. 1999. *Is Multiculturalism Bad for Women?* Princeton, NJ: Princeton University Press.

Ortbals, Candice, and Meg Rincker. 2009. "Embodied Researchers: Gendered Bodies, Research Activity, and Pregnancy in the Field." *PS: Political Science & Politics* 42 (2): 315–319.

Pachirat, Timothy. 2009. "The Political in Political Ethnography: Dispatches from the Kill Floor." In *Political Ethnography*, edited by Edward Schatz, 143–162. Chicago: University of Chicago Press.

Pachirat, Timothy. 2011. *Every Twelve Seconds: Industrialized Slaughter and the Politics of Sight.* New Haven: Yale University Press.

Pachirat, Timothy. 2012. "Working Undercover in a Slaughterhouse: An Interview with Timothy Pachirat." March 8, 2012. http://boingboing.net/2012/03/08/working-undercover-in-a-slaugh.html.

Pachirat, Timothy. 2018. *Among Wolves: Ethnography and the Immersive Study of Power.* New York: Routledge.

Parashar, Swati. 2010. "The Sacred and the Sacrilegious: Exploring Women's 'Politics' and 'Agency' in Radical Religious Movements in South Asia." *Totalitarian Movements and Political Religions* 11 (3–4): 435–55.

Parekh, Bikhu. 2000. *Rethinking Multiculturalism: Cultural Diversity and Political Theory.* Basingstoke: Macmillan.

Pateman, Carole. 1988. *The Sexual Contract.* Cambridge: Polity Press.

Pateman, Carole. 1989. *The Disorder of Women.* Stanford, CA: Stanford University Press.

Paxton, Pamela. 2000. "Women's Suffrage in the Measurement of Democracy: Problems of Operationalization." *Studies in Comparative International Development* 35 (3): 92–111.

Phoenix, Ann, and Pamela Pattynama. 2006. "Editorial." *European Journal of Women's Studies* 13 (3): 187–192.

Pokharel, Krishna, Saurabh Chaturvedi, Vibhuti Agarwal, and Tripti Lahiri. 2013. "New Delhi Attack: The Victim's Story." *Wall Street Journal*, January 9, 2013. http://www.wsj.com/articles/SB10001424127887323482504578227751166162988.

Puar, Jasbir. 2007. *Terrorist Assemblages: Homonationalism in Queer Times.* Durham, NC: Duke University Press.

Purewal, Navtej. 2010. *Son Preference: Sex Selection, Gender and Culture in South Asia.* Oxford: Berg.

Purewal, Navtej. 2014. "Disciplining the Sex Ratio: Exploring the Governmentality of Female Foeticide in India." *Identities: Global Studies in Culture and Power* 21 (5): 1–15.

Puri, Harish K. 2003. "Sikhism Scheduled Castes in Sikh Community: A Historical Perspective." *Economic and Political Weekly* 38 (26): 2693–2701.

Rai, Shirin. 1994. "Gender and Democratization: Or What Does Democracy Mean for Women in the Third World?" *Democratization* 1 (1): 209–228.

Rai, Shirin. 1996. "Women and the State in the Third World: Some Issue for Debate." In *Women and State International Perspectives,* edited by Shirin Rai and Geraldine Lievesley, 5–22. London: Taylor & Francis.

Rai, Shirin, and Geraldine Lievesley. 1996. "Introduction." In *Women and State International Perspectives,* edited by Shirin Rai and Geraldine Lievesley, 1–4. London: Taylor & Francis.

Rajivan, Anuradha. 2010. *Power, Voices, and Rights: A Turning Point for Gender Equality in Asia and the Pacific*. New Delhi: Macmillan.

Rao, Shakuntala. 2014. "Covering Rape in Shame Culture: Studying Journalism Ethics in India's New Television News Media." *Journal of Mass Media Ethics* 29: 153–167.

Raymond, Leigh, and S. Laurel Weldon. 2014. "Mini-symposium Introduction: Informal Institutions and 'Intractable' Global Problems." *Political Research Quarterly* 67 (1): 181–182.

Raymond, Leigh, S. Laurel Weldon, Daniel Kelly, Ximena B. Arriaga, and Ann Marie Clark. 2014. "Making Change: Norm-Based Strategies for Institutional Change to Address Intractable Problems." *Political Research Quarterly* 67 (1): 197–211.

Rinaldo, Rachel. 2014. "Pious and Critical: Muslim Women Activists and the Question of Agency." *Gender & Society* 28 (6): 824–46.

Robinson, Rowena. 2010. "Boundary Battles: Muslim Women and Community Identity in the Aftermath of Violence." *Women's Studies International Forum* 33: 365–373.

Rocco, Raymond. 2004. "Transforming Citizenship: Membership, Strategies of Containment and the Public Sphere in Latino Communities." *Latino Studies* 2: 4–25.

Rocco, Raymond. 2014. *Transforming Citizenship: Democracy, Membership, and Belonging in Latino Communities*. East Lansing, MI: Michigan State University Press.

Roediger, David. 1991. *The Wages of Whiteness: Race and the Making of the American Working Class*. London: Verso.

Roy, Anupama. 2014. "Gender and Citizenship in India." In *Routledge Handbook of Gender in South Asia*, edited by Leela Fernandes, 55–69. New York: Routledge.

Roy, Beth. 1994. *Some Trouble with Cows: Making Sense of Social Conflict*. Berkeley: University of California Press.

Roychowdhury, Poulami. 2013. "The Delhi Gang Rape: The Making of International Causes." *Feminist Studies* 39 (1): 282–292.

Rudolph, Susanne. 2005. "Imperialism of Categories: Situating Knowledge in a Globalizing World." *Perspectives in Politics* 3 (1): 5–14.

Rudolph, Susanne, and Lloyd Rudolph. 2000. "Living with Difference in India." *Political Quarterly* 71 (1): 20–38.

Sachdev, Chhavi. 2016. "Rape Is a Crime in India—but There Are Exceptions." NPR, April 13, 2016. http://www.npr.org/sections/goatsandsoda/2016/04/13/473966857/rape-is-a-crime-in-india-with-one-exception.

Sahni, Mohit, Neeraj Verma, D. Narula, Raji Mathew Varghese, V. Sreenivas, and Jacob Puliyel. 2008. "Missing Girls in India: Infanticide, Feticide and Made-to-Order Pregnancies? Insights from Hospital-Based Sex-Ratio-at-Birth over the Last Century." *PLoS ONE* 3 (5): e2224.

Sampaio, Anna. 2015. *Terrorizing Latina/o Immigrants: Race, Gender, and Immigration Politics in the Age of Security*. Philadelphia: Temple University Press.

Sangari, Kumkum, and Sudesh Vaid. 1999a. *Recasting Women: Essays in India Colonial History*. New Brunswick, NJ: Rutgers University Press.

Sangari, Kumkum, and Sudesh Vaid. 1999b. "Institutions, Beliefs, Ideologies: Widow Immolation in Contemporary Rajasthan." In *Gender and Politics in India*, edited by Nivedita Menon, 383–440. Oxford: Oxford University Press.

Sangtin Writers and Richa Nagar. 2006. *Playing with Fire: Feminist Thought and Activism through Seven Lives in India*. Minneapolis: University of Minnesota Press.

Sarkar, Tanika. 2001. *Hindu Wife, Hindu Nation: Community, Religion, and Cultural Nationalism*. Bloomington: Indiana University Press.

Scott, James. 1985. *Weapons of the Weak*. New Haven: Yale University Press.

Scott, James. 1989. "Forms of Everyday Resistance." *Copenhagen Journal of Asian Studies* 4: 33–62.

Scott, James. 1990. *Domination and the Arts of Resistance*. New Haven: Yale University Press.

Schatz, Edward. 2009. "Introduction: Ethnographic Immersion and the Study of Politics." In *Political Ethnography*, edited by Edward Schatz, 1–22. Chicago: University of Chicago Press.

Schwartz-Shea, Peregrine. 2006. "Judging Quality: Evaluative Criteria and Epistemic Communities." In *Interpretation and Method: Empirical Research Methods and the Interpretive Turn*, edited by Dvora Yanow and Peregrine Schwartz-Shea, 89–113. Armonk, NY: M.E. Sharpe.

Schwartz-Shea, Peregrine, and Samantha Majic. 2017. "Ethnography and Participant Observation: Political Science Research in This 'Late Methodological Moment.'" *PS: Political Science & Politics* 50 (1): 97–102.

Schwartz-Shea, Peregrine, and Dvora Yanow. 2012. *Interpretive Research Design: Concepts and Processes*. New York: Routledge.

Schweik, Susan. 2009. *The Ugly Laws: Disability in Public*. New York: New York University Press.

Schweik, Susan. 2011. "Disability and the Normal Body of the (Native) Citizen." *Social Research* 78 (2): 417–442.

Seidelman, Raymond, and Edward Harpham. 1985. *Disenchanted Realists: Political Science and the American Crisis, 1884–1994*. Albany: State University of New York Press.

Sekhon, Joti. 2006. "Engendering Grassroots Democracy: Research, Training, and Networking for Women in Local Self-Governance in India." *NWSA Journal* 118 (2): 101–122.

Sen, Amartya. 1992. "Missing Women: Social Inequality Outweighs Women's Survival Advantage in Asia and North Africa." *British Medical Journal* 304 (6827): 587–588.

Sen, Amartya. 2003. "Missing Women—Revisited: Reduction in Female Mortality Has Been Counterbalanced by Sex Selective Abortions." *British Medical Journal* 327: 1297–1298.

Shanker, Rajkumari. 2002. "Women in Sikhism." In *Women in Indian Religions*, edited by Arvind Sharma, 108–133. New Delhi: Oxford University Press.

Sharma, Amol, Vibhuti Agarwal, and Aditi Malhotra. 2013. "In Delhi Rape, New Details about Accused." *Wall Street Journal*, January 20, 2013. http://www.wsj.com/articles/SB10001424127887324081704578233762362733262.

Sharma, Betwa. 2013. "A Year Later, Family of Delhi Gang Rape Victim Press for 'Full Justice.'" *New York Times*, December 16, 2013. http://india.blogs.nytimes.com/2013/12/16/a-year-later-family-of-delhi-gang-rape-victim-press-for-full-justice/.

Shehata, Samer. 2006. "Ethnography, Identity and the Production of Knowledge." In *Interpretation and Method: Empirical Research Methods and the Interpretive*

Turn, edited by Dvora Yanow and Peregrine Schwartz-Shea, 244–263. Armonk, New York: M.E. Sharpe.

Shepherd, Laura. 2007. "'Victims, Perpetrators and Actors' Revisited: Exploring the Potential for a Feminist Reconceptualisation of (International) Security and (Gender) Violence." *British Journal of Politics and International Relations* 9 (2): 239–256.

Siim, Birte. 2000. *Gender and Citizenship: Politics and Agency in France, Britain and Denmark*. Singapore: Cambridge University Press.

Siim, Birte. 2013. "Citizenship." In *The Oxford University Handbook of Gender and Politics*, edited by Georgina Waylen, Karen Celis, Johanna Kantola, and S. Laurel Weldon, 756–780. Oxford: Oxford University Press.

Siim, Birte. 2014. "Political Intersectionality and Democratic Politics in European Public Sphere." *Politics & Gender* 10 (1): 117–124.

Singh, Gurnam. 2006. "Sikhism's Emancipatory Discourses: Some Critical Perspectives." *Sikh Formations* 2 (2): 135–151.

Singh, I. J. 1998. *Sikhs and Sikhism: A View with a Bias*. Guelph: Centennial Foundation.

Singh, Jakeet. 2015. "Religious Agency and the Limits of Intersectionality." *Hypatia* 30 (4): 657–674.

Singh, Nikky Guninder Kaur. 1993. *The Feminine Principle in the Sikh Vision of the Transcendent*. Cambridge: Cambridge University Press.

Singh, Nikky Guninder Kaur. 2000. "Why Did I Not Light the Fire? The Refeminization of Ritual in Sikhism." *Journal of Feminist Studies in Religion* 16 (1): 63–85.

Singh, Nikky Guninder Kaur. 2008. "Re-imagining the Divine in Sikhism." *Feminist Theology* 16 (3): 332–349.

Singh, Nikky Guninder Kaur. 2009. "Female Feticide in the Punjab and Fetus Imagery in Sikhism." In *Imagining the Fetus*, edited by Vanessa Sasson and Jane Marie Law, 121–136. Oxford: Oxford University Press.

Singh, Pashaura. 2014. "An Overview of Sikh History." In *The Oxford Handbook of Sikh Studies*, edited by Pashaura Singh and Louis Fenech, 19–34. Oxford: Oxford University Press.

Smith, Rogers. 1989. "'One United People': Second-Class Female Citizenship and the American Quest for Community." *Yale Journal of Law and the Humanities* 1: 229–293.

Somit, Albert, and Joseph Tanenhaus. 1967. *The Development of Political Science: From Burgess to Behaviorism*. Boston: Allyn and Bacon.

Soss, Joe. 2002. *Unwanted Claims: The Politics of Participation in the U.S. Welfare System*. Ann Arbor: University of Michigan Press.

Sprague, Joey. 2005. *Feminist Methodologies for Critical Researchers: Bridging Differences*. Walnut Creek, CA: Altamira.

Subramanian, Narendra. 2014. *Nation and Family: Personal Law, Cultural Pluralism, and Gendered Citizenship in India*. Stanford, CA: Stanford University Press.

"Sukhmani Sahib Sewa Society Turns 50." *The Tribune*, September 22, 2015. http://www.tribuneindia.com/article/news_print.aspx?story_id=135978&catid=20&mid=53.

Sunder Rajan, Rajeswari. 2000. "Women between Community and State: Some Implications of the Uniform Civil Code Debates in India." *Social Text* 18 (4): 56–82.

Sunder Rajan, Rajeswari. 2003. *The Scandal of the State: Women, Law, and Citizenship in Postcolonial India*. Durham, NC: Duke University Press.

Thomson Reuters Foundation. 2017. Survey of the World's Most Dangerous Cities for Women. http://poll2017.trust.org/city/?id=delhi.

Thomson Reuters Foundation. 2018. Survey of the World's Most Dangerous Countries for Women. http://poll2018.trust.org/.

Tickner, J. Ann. 2006. "Feminism Meets International Relations: Some Methodological Issues." In *Feminist Methodologies for International Relations*, edited by Brooke Ackerly, Maria Stern, and Jacqui True, 19–41. Cambridge: Cambridge University Press.

Tickner, J. Ann. 2015. "Revisiting IR in a Time of Crisis." *International Feminist Journal of Politics* 17 (4): 536–553.

Townsend-Bell, Erica. 2009. "Being True and Being You: Race, Gender, Class, and the Fieldwork Experience." *PS: Political Science & Politics* 42 (2): 311–314.

Townsend-Bell, Erica. 2011. "What Is Relevance? Defining Intersectional Praxis in Uruguay." *Political Research Quarterly* 64 (1): 187–199.

Townsend-Bell, Erica. 2014. "Ambivalent Intersectionality." *Politics & Gender* 10 (1): 137–142.

Tripp, Aili. 2013. "Political Systems and Gender." In *The Oxford University Handbook of Gender and Politics*, edited by Georgina Waylen, Karen Celis, Johanna Kantola, and S. Laurel Weldon, 514–535. Oxford: Oxford University Press.

Trivedi, Lisa. 2003. "Women in India." In *Understanding Contemporary India*, edited by Neil DeVotta and Sumit Ganguly, 181–208. Boulder, CO: Lynne Rienner.

True, Jacqui. 2015. "Winning the Battle but Losing the War on Violence." *International Feminist Journal of Politics* 17 (4): 554–572.

Tully, James. 1995. *Strange Multiplicity: Constitutionalism in an Age of Diversity*. Cambridge: Cambridge University Press.

Turner, Bryan. 1990. "Outline of a Theory of Citizenship." *Sociology* 24 (2): 189–217.

Twine, France Winddance, and Jonathan Warren. 2000. *Racing Research, Researching Race: Methodological Dilemmas in Critical Race Studies*. New York: New York University Press.

United Nations Office on Drugs and Crime. 2010. *International Statistics on Crime and Justice*. Helsinki: HEUNI Publication.

United Nations Women. 2012. Survey, Safer Cities Free of Violence against Women and Girls Initiative.

United Nations Women. 2014. *Sex Ratios and Gender Biased Sex Selection: History, Debates, and Future Directions*. New Delhi: UN Women.

Unni, Jeemol. 1999. "Property Rights for Women: Case for Joint Titles to Agricultural Land and Urban Housing." *Economic and Political Weekly* 34 (21): 1281–1286.

Verma, J. S., Leila Seth, and Gopal Subramanium. 2013. *Report of the Committee on Amendments to Criminal Law*. New Delhi: PRS Legislative Research.

Wadsworth, Nancy. 2011. "Intersectionality in California's Same-Sex Marriage Battles: A Complex Proposition." *Political Research Quarterly* 64 (1): 200–216.

Walsh, Denise. 2012. "Does the Quality of Democracy Matter for Women's Rights? Just Debate and Democratic Transition in Chile and South Africa." *Comparative Political Studies* 45 (11): 1323–1350.

Walsh, Shannon, and Cecilia Menjivar. 2016a. "Impunity and Multisided Violence in the Lives of Latin American Women: El Salvador in Comparative Perspective." *Current Sociology* 64 (4): 586–602.

Walsh, Shannon, and Cecilia Menjivar. 2016b. "What Guarantees Do We Have?" Legal Tolls and Persistent Impunity for Feminicide in Guatemala. *Latin American Politics and Society* 58 (4): 31–55.

Walzer, Michael. 1989. "Citizenship." In *Political Innovation and Conceptual Change*, edited by Terence Ball, James Farr, and Russell L. Hanson, 211–219. Cambridge: Cambridge University Press.

Walzer, Michael. 1991. "The Idea of Civil Society." *Dissent* 38 (2): 293–304.

Waylen, Georgina. 2007. *Engendering Transitions: Women's Mobilization, Institutions and Gender Outcomes.* Oxford: Oxford University Press.

Waylen, Georgina. 2014. "Informal Institutions, Institutional Change, and Gender Equality." *Political Research Quarterly* 67 (1): 212–223.

Waylen, Georgina, Karen Celis, Johanna Kantola, and S. Laurel Weldon, eds. 2013. *The Oxford University Handbook of Gender and Politics.* Oxford: Oxford University Press.

Weldon, S. Laurel. 2002. *Protest, Policy, and the Problem of Violence against Women.* Pittsburgh: University of Pittsburgh Press.

Weldon, S. Laurel. 2004. "The Dimensions and Policy Impact of Feminist Civil Society." *International Feminist Journal of Politics* 6 (1): 1–28.

Weldon, S. Laurel. 2013. "Dialogue: New Approaches to Thinking about Power and the Political?" *Politics, Groups, and Identities* 1 (1): 85–118.

West, Cornel. 1988. "CLS and a Liberal Critic." *Yale Law Journal* 97 (5): 757–771.

West, Cornel. 1995. "Foreword." In *Critical Race Theory: The Key Writings That Formed the Movement*, edited by Kimberlé Crenshaw, Neil Gotanda, Gary Peller, and Kendall Thomas, xi–xii. New York: New Press.

Wikan, Unni. 2002. *Generous Betrayal: Politics of Culture in the New Europe.* Chicago: Chicago University Press.

Williams, Patricia. 1991. *The Alchemy of Race and Rights.* Cambridge, MA: Harvard University Press.

Williams, Rina Verma. 2006. *Postcolonial Politics and Personal Laws: Colonial Legacies and the Indian State.* New York: Oxford University Press.

Yuval-Davis, Nira. 1997. "Women, Citizenship and Difference." *Feminist Review* 57: 4–27.

Yuval-Davis, Nira. 2006a. "Intersectionality and Feminist Politics." *European Journal of Women's Studies* 13 (3): 193–209.

Yuval-Davis, Nira. 2006b. "Belonging and the Politics of Belonging." *Patterns of Prejudice* 40 (3): 197–214.

Yuval-Davis, Nira, and Pnina Werbner. 1999. *Women, Citizenship and Difference.* London: Zed Books.

Zirakzadeh, Cyrus Ernesto. 2009. "When Nationalists Are Not Separatists: Discarding and Recovering Academic Theories While Doing Fieldwork in the Basque Region of Spain." In *Political Ethnography*, edited by Edward Schatz, 97–118. Chicago: University of Chicago Press.

CPSIA information can be obtained
at www.ICGtesting.com
Printed in the USA
BVHW030002271121
622639BV00003B/128